Touchdown: The Development of Propulsion Controlled Aircraft at NASA Dryden

by
Tom Tucker

NASA History Office
Office of Policy and Plans
NASA Headquarters
Washington, DC 20546

Monographs in
Aerospace History
Number 16
1999

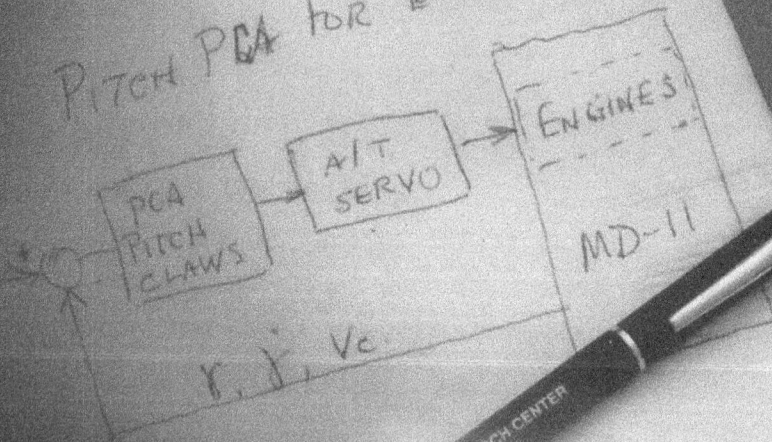

Table of Contents

Foreword iv

Preface v

The Development of Propulsion Controlled Aircraft at NASA Dryden 1

Appendices

    Appendix A: Aircraft Accident Report, United Airlines Flight 232 36

    Appendix B: Flight Simulator Studies 38

    Appendix C: National Transportation Safety Board Recommendation 39

    Appendix D: Guest Pilot Comments on . . . F-15 40

    Appendix E: PCA System Landing in MD-11 Aircraft 46

    Appendix F: Summary of Guest Pilot Comments about . . . MD-11 47

    Appendix G: Awards and Honors [for the PCA Team] 50

Index 51

About the Author 54

Foreword

This monograph relates the important history of the Propulsion Controlled Aircraft project at NASA's Dryden Flight Research Center. Spurred by a number of airplane crashes caused by the loss of hydraulic flight controls, a NASA-industry team lead by Frank W. Burcham and C. Gordon Fullerton developed a way to land an aircraft safely using only engine thrust to control the airplane.

In spite of initial skepticism, the team discovered that, by manually manipulating an airplane's thrust, there was adequate control for extended up-and-away flight. However, there was not adequate control precision for safe runway landings because of the small control forces, slow response, and difficulty in damping the airplane phugoid and Dutch roll oscillations. The team therefore conceived, developed, and tested the first computerized Propulsion Controlled Aircraft (PCA) system. The PCA system takes pilot commands, uses feedback from airplane measurements, and computes commands for the thrust of each engine, yielding much more precise control. Pitch rate and velocity feedback damp the phugoid oscillation, while yaw rate feedback damps the Dutch roll motion.

The team tested the PCA system in simulators and conducted flight research in F-15 and MD-11 airplanes. Later, they developed less sophisticated variants of PCA called PCA Lite and PCA Ultralite to make the system cheaper and therefore more attractive to industry. This monograph tells the PCA story in a non-technical way with emphasis on the human aspects of the engineering and flight-research effort. It thereby supplements the extensive technical literature on PCA and makes the development of this technology accessible to a wide audience. I commend this brief account to anyone interested in the progress of aviation technology.

Kevin L. Petersen
Director, Dryden Flight Research Center
18 February 1999

Preface

Many histories of invention look back over decades and even centuries to tell their tale. But another perspective comes from the middle of the process, when the outcome is uncertain, when questions remain, when the invention and development process remain a "hazard of fortune." It is a rewarding experience to view developing technology from this angle. The story of the invention and development of Propulsion Controlled Aircraft at NASA Dryden Flight Research Center made this point again and again to me in the summer of 1998 as I researched the invention within several hundred yards of where only several years before, the first jumbo jet lumbered in for a safe landing using the new technology.

I owe a great debt to the many individuals, programs, and organizations which enabled me to write this history. First, I am grateful to the NASA - ASEE Summer Faculty Fellowship Program which brought me to NASA Dryden Flight Research Center out in the Mojave Desert and supplied me with every kind of support needed for research and writing. At Dryden Center, Don Black and Kristie Carlson provided much courtesy and good advice. At the Stanford University Department of Aeronautics and Astronautics, Melinda Francis Gratteau, Program Administrator, and Michael Tauber, Co-director of the Program, aided me invaluably with their help, consideration, and provision of opportunities. The participatory programs they offered to me and other NASA ASEE fellows at the NASA Ames Research Center helped me in thinking about and clarifying this invention history project.

Many people inside and outside NASA gave generously of their time and expertise in interviews and correspondence. These included: Russ Barber, Bob Baron, John Bull, Bill Burcham, John Burken, Joe Conley, Bill Dana, Dwain Deets, Michael Dornheim, John Feather, Dennis Fitch, Gordon Fullerton, Glenn Gilyard, Al Haynes, Tom Imrich, Jeff Kahler, Yvonne Kellogg, John Lauber, Jeannette Le, Trindel Maine, John Miller, Terry Neighbor, Drew Pappas, Dana Purifoy, Joel Sitz, Walt Smith, Jim Smolka, Jim Stewart, Ken Szalai, Jim Urness, Tom Wolf, and Bob Yeager.

Readers of drafts along the way offered many valuable comments. I especially thank: Bill Burcham, Roger Launius, Trindel Maine, and John Miller. I am grateful to Dennis Ragsdale of the NASA Dryden Library for tracking down my numerous research requests. Steven Lighthill and the NASA Dryden Graphics Department as well as the NASA Dryden Photo Lab went above and beyond the call of duty in giving this project the benefit of their talents. Camilla McArthur deserves recognition for her expert work arranging for the printing of the monograph through the Government Printing Office.

Last and most, I owe a debt to Dill Hunley, chief editor, advisor, facilitator, and friend who throughout the process made this history much better than it could have been through my efforts alone.

Tom Tucker
Spindale, NC
12 April 1999

Touchdown: The Development of Propulsion Controlled Aircraft at NASA Dryden

At 30,000 feet altitude flying to St. Louis on a business trip, Bill Burcham, then Chief Propulsion Engineer at NASA's Dryden Flight Research Center, had an idea that would change his life. It was a late summer day in 1989. Burcham pushed aside his well-thumbed copy of the trade journal *Aviation Week & Space Technology*. As the peaceful routine of the commercial flight went on, he began to draw. He began a sketch on the back of a TWA cocktail napkin.

Burcham, a thirty-three year veteran in aeronautics at NASA, is well-known to his colleagues as a man whose emotions even in emergency never modulate beyond matter-of-fact. So there were no Eureka shouts. There was only his pen dancing over paper.

The spark that started him thinking was the latest in a series of articles appearing that summer about a major jet crash.[1] On 19 July 1989, a widebody jet had experienced disaster during a routine flight over Iowa farmlands. The rear engine had blown out. The loss of this engine's thrust was not central to the mayhem that followed. In fact, the two other engines slung under the wings remained sufficient for somewhat regular flight. But the hydraulic system had vanished. The hydraulics operate all the controls that a pilot uses to control flight. The airplane had three hydraulic systems, any two of them capable of providing almost normal control, and any one capable of providing a safe landing, but the shrapnel from the explosion had taken out all three. Suddenly, the control wheel was dead in the pilot's hand.

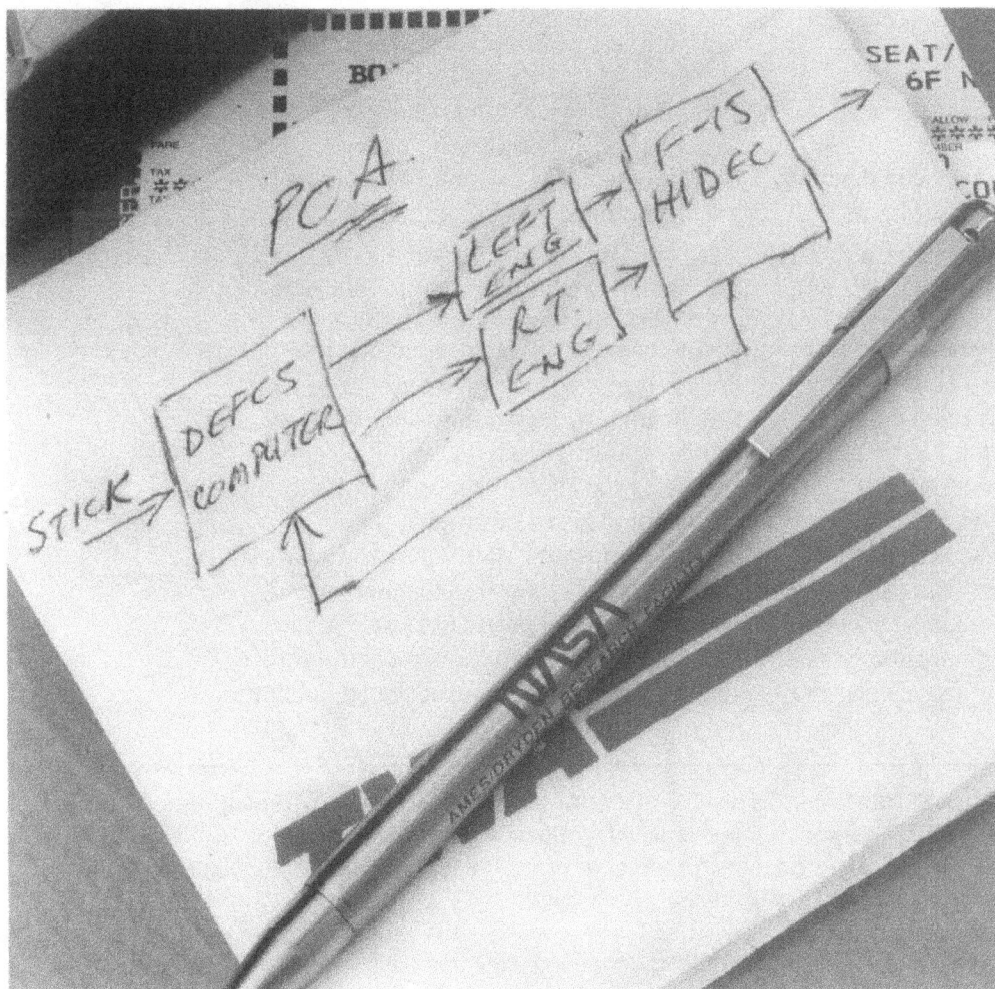

Figure 1. Bill Burcham's PCA napkin, showing the diagram of Dryden's Propulsion Controlled Aircraft project. In the diagram, DEFCS stands for Digital Electronic Flight Control System, a computerized system that provides digital flight controls; HIDEC stands for Highly Integrated Digital Electronic Control. (NASA photo EC94-42805-1 by Dennis Taylor).

[1] See Frank W. Burcham, "Cleared for Landing," *Air & Space* (April/May 1995): 20-21.

As the plane moved bizarrely across the sky and the flight attendants wheeled back meal carts unserved and passengers stirred uneasily, the crew wrestled with the problem of landing the airplane. Captain Al Haynes and Dennis Fitch, an airline check pilot who had hurried forward to help in the cockpit, made a discovery. By nudging the throttles to the

an idea big enough perhaps to prevent similar disasters in the future.

What he scratched down was a schematic diagram.[3] He showed his drawing to project manager Jim Stewart, the friend and NASA associate seated next to him. They bounced concepts back and forth. "He thought it was a great idea," remem-

Figure 2. The F-15 flown in the HIDEC program and also PCA. (NASA photo EC86-33538-2 Fr23 by Mike Smith).

two remaining engines, they could herd the airplane across the skies. Flight controllers contacted the crew and directed the airplane to the Sioux Gateway Airport at Sioux City, where emergency preparations had already begun. At 1600 hours, the airliner made a crash landing on Runway 22. It cartwheeled during touchdown, yet 184 of the 296 on board survived the crash and ensuing fire.[2]

"Could I come up with something that would have helped those fellows?" Burcham remembers thinking. He continued to sketch on the napkin. On the four-inch-square plane of soft tissue appeared

bers Burcham, "and within five minutes we had outlined a test program."[4]

His idea was a backup landing technique for an airplane that has lost all normal flight controls. Burcham wondered if he could maneuver a crippled airplane to a safe landing by harnessing the brute force of the engines. He would exploit some technology available in recent airplanes. These new aircraft had digital flight control computers. They also had digital engine control computers that ran the engines. Why not program these digital computers to provide enough control for a touchdown? At that time, educated opinion

---

[2] See David Hughes and Michael Dornheim, "United DC-10 Crashes in Sioux City, Iowa," *Aviation Week & Space Technology* (24 July 1989): 96-97; National Transportation Safety Board Aircraft Accident Report, *United Airlines Flight 232, McDonnell Douglas DC-10-10, Sioux Gateway Airport, Sioux City, Iowa, July 19,1989* (Washington, DC, 1989). Appendix A of this monograph reproduces details from the latter source.

[3] Frank W. Burcham, interview with author, 15 June 1998, as well as 6 other interviews with author over summer of 1998.

[4] Burcham interview, 15 June 1998.

would have been that if you tried to land an airplane on a runway with this technology, you would end up with a smoking hole in the ground.

* * *

Out in the Mojave Desert 70 miles northeast of Los Angeles are the plain offices, metal shacks, and hangars that comprise the NASA Dryden Flight Research Center on Edwards Air Force Base. The ancient dry lakebed gleams in the afternoon sun as if it were a fantastic illustration for a science fiction paperback. But even more paradoxical are the

along in an hour snatched at the end of a week. Or after a day's flight, he would call the research pilot and in his affable, low-key manner inquire, "Gotta hundred pounds of extra gas; could you try this backup card test point?" The researchers have names for this type of investigation—they call it "bootlegging" or "piggybacking" or "in the noise" (an engineer's term for experimental efforts so minimal they can be neglected). No dramatic leaps greeted this effort, which was to become for Burcham something near a quest. The path was evolution rather than revolution.

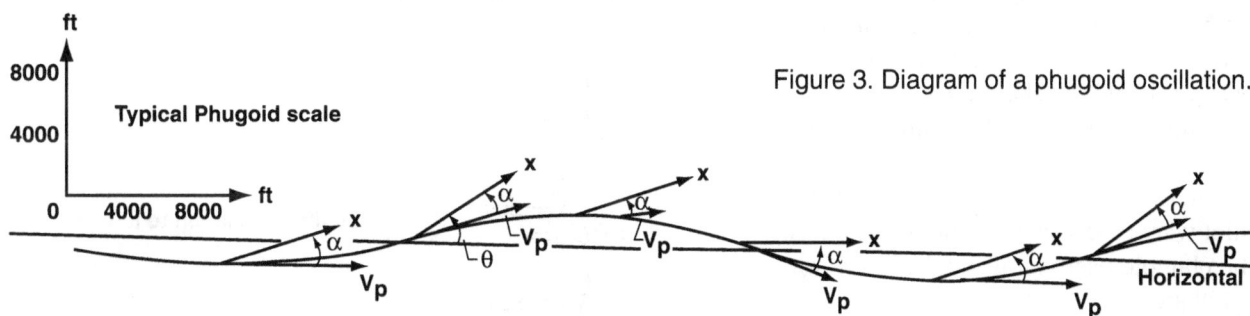

Figure 3. Diagram of a phugoid oscillation.

labs and offices where on battered federal desks dating back two generations, concepts for use in the aircraft of the next millennium are born and developed. Despite NASA's charter commitment to commercial air safety innovation, it was also, by many standards, a strange site for Burcham's idea.[5]

The napkin scheme did not initially come to life with the dignity of a project with a budget, but for months Burcham pushed it

Stewart and Burcham had been exploring a new technology known as HIDEC, Highly Integrated Digital Electronic Control, an attempt to optimize engine performance to match the flight conditions of the aircraft by integrating engine and flight control systems. A follow-on activity involved doing on-board diagnostics when an airplane was damaged and then reconfiguring what remained functional to fly the airplane.[6]

---

[5] Although NASA's Dryden Flight Research Center and its predecessor organizations have an illustrious history of flight research on a wide variety of aircraft, other NASA centers have traditionally been more closely associated with transport technology.

[6] Despite the temptation to trace connections between HIDEC and Burcham's new project for landing aircraft with engine control—which came to be called Propulsion Controlled Aircraft (see below in narrative)—and to view the earlier project as a conceptual starting point for the later one, these are quite distinct programs. In editorial notes to this text, Dryden engineer Trindel Maine cautioned, "HIDEC really wasn't primarily a reconfiguration program, though at least one reconfiguration program was flown under its auspices. Primarily it was a series of experiments designed to discover and demonstrate the benefits of going to computer-controlled engines. This included a greater ability to recognize engine problems, change engine setting depending on the situation, and cut out excess operating margins."

"We had already looked at engines," recalls Stewart; "that is one thing all these planes have in common."[7] It was a glance merely, a preliminary study, no proof. But the engineers had already looked into reconfiguration enough to speculate that if more than one control surface did not function, the airplane was in trouble. To lose them all and depend on engine thrust alone would be, in effect, the ultimate reconfiguration. In the pantheon of bad-case scenarios, this was the worst.

Passengers on a commercial flight may instinctively sense that destiny is in the control of the big engines, the big airframe. But the most crucial parts are the narrow metal strips: the ailerons on the back of the wings, the rudder, and the elevators on the back of the tail fins that control flightpath. These strips also dominate certain unbalanced motions no pilot wants unleashed, motions known as the phugoid oscillation and the Dutch roll oscillation.

You experience phugoid oscillations in almost any air flight. They probably make an appearance as no more than slight nibbles in a smooth passage, arising so gradually that normally the pilot touches the wheel and kills the oscillation without thinking about it.

The phugoid is a pitching motion in which kinetic and potential energy (speed and altitude) are traded. Each cycle of the oscillation typically lasts about 60 seconds and may continue for many minutes. As the airplane's nose pitches to

the highest point, speed slows. As the nose drops back toward the middle of the cycle, speed increases. The experience resembles a sort of eerie slow-motion roller coaster ride. Its effect on landings can be fatal if the motion continues uncontrolled near the ground.

The second oscillation is known as the Dutch roll (named for the motion of an ice skater). According to one NASA research pilot, an airplane in the Dutch roll mode "resembles a snake slithering."[8] Obviously, this is not a desirable way to travel off the ground. This complex oscillation combines several factors including yaw, roll, dihedral effect, lift, and drag. In a

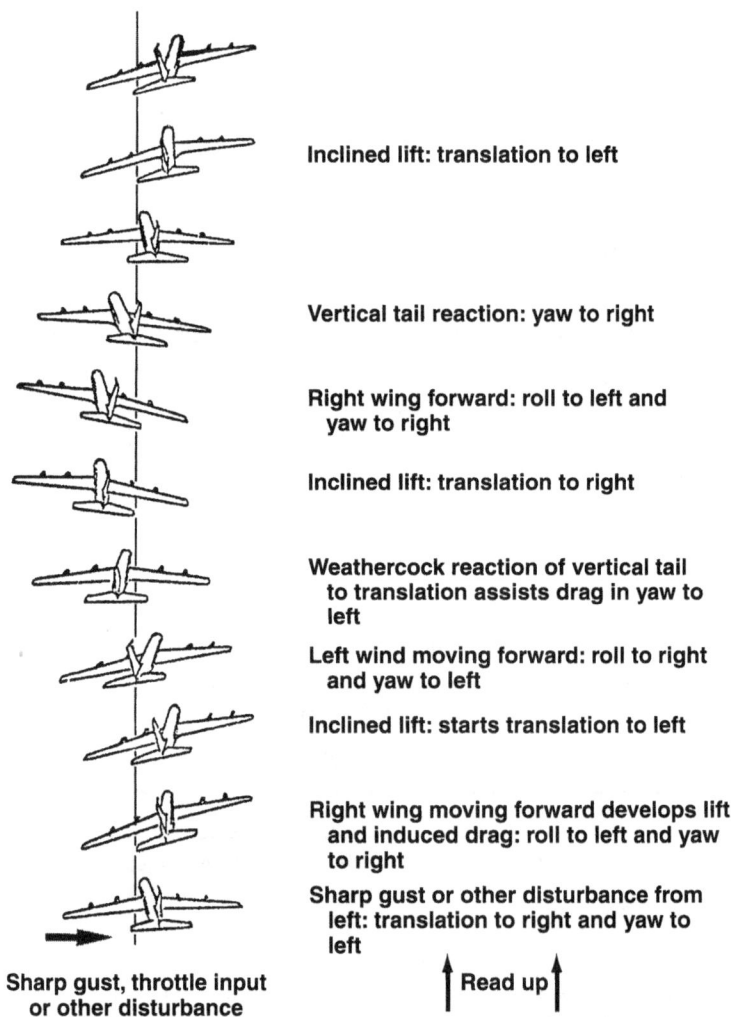

Figure 4. Diagram of a Dutch roll.

Inclined lift: translation to left

Vertical tail reaction: yaw to right

Right wing forward: roll to left and yaw to right

Inclined lift: translation to right

Weathercock reaction of vertical tail to translation assists drag in yaw to left

Left wind moving forward: roll to right and yaw to left

Inclined lift: starts translation to left

Right wing moving forward develops lift and induced drag: roll to left and yaw to right

Sharp gust or other disturbance from left: translation to right and yaw to left

Sharp gust, throttle input or other disturbance

↑ Read up ↑

[7] James Stewart, interview with author, 10 June 1998.

[8] Dana Purifoy, interview with author, 2 July 1998.

Dutch roll, the airplane's nose typically rotates through about three degrees. When an airplane tries to find the runway, there is only about one degree of margin for safe runway touchdowns.[9]

Although concern with these mysterious oscillations lay on the horizon before Burcham's technology, the project had a clear, specific goal—to land a jumbo jet using engine thrust alone. None of the in-between steps were well defined and some would not, as it turned out, resolve themselves for years. Any proposed change to passenger aircraft requires endless refining tests, proof upon proof to check the vast web of real flight possibility. The Federal Aviation Administration (FAA), the National Transportation Safety Board (NTSB), the manufacturer, the airlines, and various associations and advisory groups are all part of the mesh. But the unknowns stretched beyond regular procedures. "We had to ask basic questions," recalls Jim Stewart. "Can you control the airplane [this way]? And some here were saying *no*."[10]

Burcham had already devised an acronym for the project. The typical NASA project generates several acronyms in its lifetime. To outsiders, the engineers who coin these names may seem like techies taking their revenge on the English language. The acronyms are born and die—few of them ever survive as standard usage, and they sometimes change on the same project from report to report. You need a scorecard to read these reports, continually referring to the inevitable "Nomenclature" section appearing on page one right beneath the "Abstract." Along the

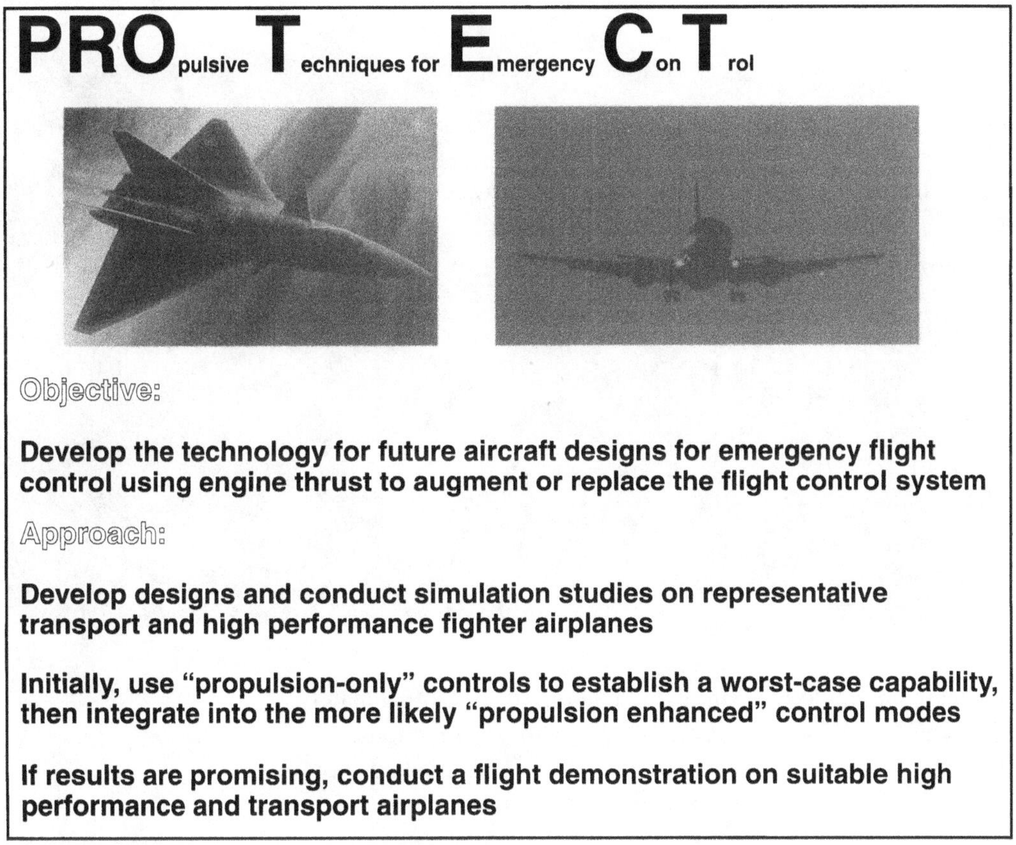

PROpulsive **T**echniques for **E**mergency **C**on**T**rol

Objective:

Develop the technology for future aircraft designs for emergency flight control using engine thrust to augment or replace the flight control system

Approach:

Develop designs and conduct simulation studies on representative transport and high performance fighter airplanes

Initially, use "propulsion-only" controls to establish a worst-case capability, then integrate into the more likely "propulsion enhanced" control modes

If results are promising, conduct a flight demonstration on suitable high performance and transport airplanes

Figure 5. An early acronym and also a sample of Bill Burcham's viewgraph expertise

---

[9] See Donna Gerren, "Design, Analysis, and Control of Large Transport Aircraft utilizing Engine Thrust as a Backup System for the Primary Flight Controls" (unpublished thesis, University of Kansas, Feb. 1993): 20-22. This thesis was later published as NASA CR-186035 in October of 1995.

[10] Stewart interview.

way the project was known as PROTECT (PROpulsive Techniques for Emergency ConTrol), POC (Propulsion Only Control), and PROFAC, an acronym that today causes all concerned to scratch their heads when asked to explain its forgotten origin. Marketing may be the true mainspring behind these verbalizations. A good acronym resonates. "If you don't have a good acronym," offers one engineer, "you're dead in the water."[11] The ultimate acronym, coined by industry, turned out to be PCA, Propulsion Controlled Aircraft.

The first step for PCA was to see if a pilot could alter the course of the airplane simply by working the throttles. To test

airplane that he and Burcham used as a testbed for HIDEC projects. Burcham, a skilled amateur pilot, climbed in the cockpit. First, he tried the lateral movement. Could he turn the F-15? "I found that by advancing one throttle and retarding the other," recalls Burcham, "the F-15 rolled nicely, even though the engines are close together."

Next, he pushed both throttles up a bit. When he did, the airplane nosed up slightly. If he cut both throttles back, the nose dipped. He had demonstrated some longitudinal control. In the excitement, all in a lunch hour away from his primary project, he moved on to the next step, the

Figure 6. The Dryden F-15 simulator cockpit.

this, Burcham went to veteran simulations engineer Tom Wolf. "Can you lock down all the flight controls on a sim [simulation]?" he asked.

The next morning, Wolf had the sim ready. He had altered the F-15 sim, a model of a high performance fighter

simulated landing itself. Unfortunately, his exhilarating video screen journey came to an end when he crashed short of the imaginary runway.

Burcham continued step-by-step. He was doing what Denny Fitch had done on Flight 232. He called it Throttles Only

---

[11] John Burken, interview with author, 9 June 1998.

Control (TOC).[12] It was a necessary step, not a destination. But with repeated practice, he managed to use TOC to land the F-15 in the simulation. "There seemed to be enough brute force there," he said, "that I felt with a computer providing some finesse, safe landings would be possible."[13]

* * *

Glenn Gilyard is a 55-year-old senior Dryden controls engineer who specializes in computer-assisted controls. A large man whose eyes gleam with elfin humor, he recalls his first encounter with PCA. Kevin Petersen, Chief of the Vehicle Technology Branch in the Research Engineering Division, approached him one afternoon in 1990. Despite the skepticism at the Center, Petersen was intrigued by PCA and hesitantly asked Gilyard if he would put some time into the project.

"I jumped on it right off the bat," says Gilyard, "This appeared *feasible*."

Gilyard looked at the solution as an autopilot function. He had worked on innovative solutions for the auto-throttle of the YF-12. What if he used the pilot's control stick to command direction? The input would go through the flight computer, which would also receive sensor feedback from the airplane and use it to calculate and move the throttles.

Where would they get the sim airplane to make the control tests? Although the F-15 simulation had already been used, in the corner of the lab rested another sim from an abandoned project—a four-engine

transport, the Boeing 720. There was not a real Boeing 720 waiting outside on the Edwards base runway to take investigation to the next level. Rather, it was the only transport simulation available.

Gilyard's eyes gleam with mischief when he explains why the sim but no airplane was available. Once Dryden did employ a real Boeing 720 for use in experiments. The FAA had committed a significant budget and many technicians to compound a jet fuel with a new additive intended to prevent airplanes from burning on impact. It was a wonderful idea. It had passed the reviews, the simulations, the small-scale demolition rehearsals. But the real flight was different. Later, investigation would reveal the unforeseen factor, a wing cutter slicing through an engine on impact. The airplane erupted in a giant fireball and burned for an hour.

The unhappy project had flown under the acronym CID, Controlled Impact Demonstration. Gilyard smiles, recalling that wags on the base to this day explained the acronym as "Crash In Desert."

"It burned like a blowtorch," recalls Gilyard.[14]

* * *

Now Burcham had an informal team assembled to work on PCA control laws including two newcomers, Jeanette Le, just graduated from UCLA, who would function as the sim engineer, and Joe Conley, fresh out of the engineering program at the University of Illinois and the NASA coop program, who would be responsible for the analytics. Burcham's

---

[12] The acronym TOC is important to this history. It refers to the pilot manually operating the engine throttles to provide flight control. The acronym later adopted, PCA (Propulsion Controlled Aircraft), refers to augmented controls the project developed to help the airplane land.

[13] Burcham, "Cleared for Landing," 20.

[14] Last section based on Glenn Gilyard, interview with author, 16 June 1998.

project had advanced beyond the four corners of his desk to become a training ground for two new-hires with a thrift-shop choice for its testbed.

Late in January of 1990, Gilyard sketched out the control laws. More than anyone anticipated, the first effort looked very good. Le brought up what had early-on been a more-than-adequate 720 sim and modeled it for flight using throttles for flight-path control and other multiple scenarios. Within a week, these engineers were flying the PCA system in the sim lab.

"No pilots involved at first," winks Gilyard, "no sense in embarrassing ourselves, huh? Typically it takes months and months if not years to get results. Normally, you start at your desk; you make a mathematical representation or model of the aircraft. Then you do the control law design at your desk. What we did was the exception to the rule. We jumped right into the sim."[15]

A simulation is a software model of an airplane. The model includes a maze of subsystems, the propulsion system, the control system, an aerodynamic model, an actuation model, a model typically of a specific airport and actual runway, models of weather, wind, turbulence, gusts. In effect, when you stepped into the plywood cockpit of the Dryden 720 sim, you entered an elaborate video game, an arrangement that might answer any number of speculative questions about flight but that at the same time entailed none of the risks of real flight.

The 720 sim was rough. It was a plywood box; it had only two throttles so that the sim had to tie two software engines together on the left and two on the right.

The video screen offered a tiny rectangle. The mathematics of its models had been derived for another project whose focus was crashing, instead of not-crashing. Yet the more sims Burcham saw, the more certain he became that in some manageable way, thrust would do to land an airplane.[16]

During these "quickie" formulations, another issue arose. It was not part of the propulsion control modeling. But it was part of any safe landing in a catastrophic scenario. The speed of the aircraft without normal flight controls is mostly locked into the speed flown before control was lost. An aircraft has what is called its trim airspeed, an inherent speed the airplane attempts to maintain. Speed is only peripherally affected by changing thrust. To an outsider, it might seem that if you want your car, for instance, to slow down, you take your foot off the gas pedal. But in the PCA mode, if you cut back on the throttle, you do not decrease speed—you pitch the nose down. Correspondingly, if you bring up the throttle, you pitch the nose up. The increases and decreases in angle of attack cause drag which marginally affects speed, but you face a problem: if you are flying at altitude at 280 knots and experience catastrophic loss of your normal controls, even when you engage PCA, you still fly at something unnervingly close to 280 knots. How do you slow down to perhaps the 170 knots needed for a safe landing? Here was an issue to address. But as Gilyard, the old control-law warrior, noted: his assignment at this point was done, and the flight demonstration was for others—it was, as he phrased it, "another set of realities."[17]

For the moment, the problem of trim speed could be postponed. Burcham had some promising results, and he needed

---

[15] Gilyard interview.

[16] Jeanette Le, interview with author, 24 June 1998.

[17] Gilyard interview.

every bit of confidence he could get. There were many naysayers on the topic of PCA, and the roughest criticism came from the nearest hallways. "This is just plain stupid," snorted one fellow engineer. "Hare-brained!" echoed another aeronautical designer. A Dryden expert warned him, "You are defying the laws of physics!" Skepticism was voiced from all levels, low and high. The Planning Council at Dryden did not offer funds. "By the time you had brought it up to ten people," recalls Jim Stewart who shared the early advocacy, "you almost hated to bring it up." Burcham's logbook has entries for many PCA briefings that winter which end with the notation "no interest."[18]

Why were there so many doubters? Perhaps one of the answers was cultural. In this realm of specialized research, there was a propulsion culture and a separate flight control culture. PCA was a hybrid of both that pleased traditionalists in neither. And another factor surfaces too: the whole concept of PCA was, in a large way, unsettling. An engineer now sympathetic who prides himself on openness to new ideas recalls that at first he did not think the technology would work, "PCA wasn't intuitively obvious. The problem hinged on this," his eyebrows widen for emphasis, "It was *novel*."[19]

Early in the spring, Burcham received a brief note from Ken Szalai, Director at

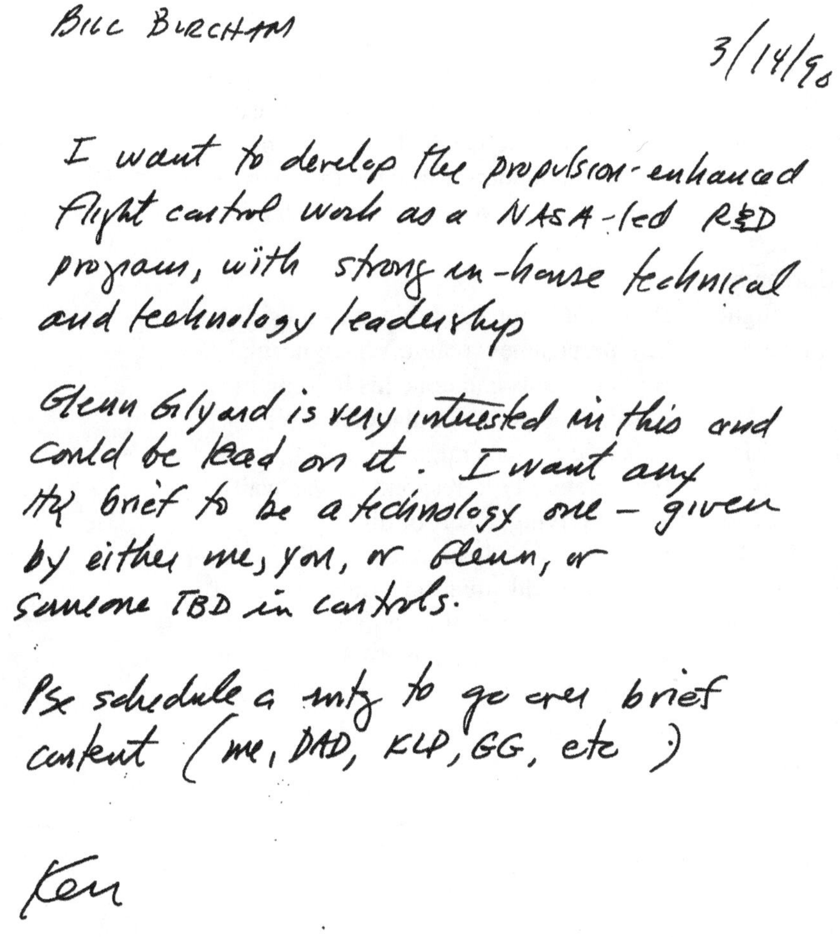

BILL BURCHAM   3/14/90

I want to develop the propulsion-enhanced flight control work as a NASA-led R&D program, with strong in-house technical and technology leadership

Glenn Gilyard is very interested in this and could be lead on it. I want any tech brief to be a technology one — given by either me, you, or Glenn, or someone TBD in controls.

Pse schedule a mtg to go over brief content (me, DAD, KLP, GG, etc)

Ken

Figure 7. Dryden Director Ken Szalai's note to Bill Burcham.

---

[18] Frank W. Burcham, unpublished log books; Stewart interview. The Jim Stewart interview with the author was one of the more extensive sources on early skepticism about PCA.

[19] Tom Wolf, interview with author 4 Aug. 1998.

NASA Dryden. Although it was informal, casually scrawled by hand, the note arrived as a real trumpet blast. "I want to develop the propulsion-enhanced flight control work as a NASA-led R&D [Research and Development] program, with strong in-house technical and technology leadership," he announced.[20] Szalai did not offer him a budget or people to stack against the project, but at this stage, what he offered may have been more essential. Szalai had received a message from NASA Headquarters in Washington, D.C. There was concern at Headquarters that PCA might excite the regulatory agencies before it had been fully explored and create problems for the aircraft manufacturers. "The advice I got from Headquarters," recalls Szalai, "was: 'We'd prefer you not actually work on this at all'—which was a stunning blow to me."[21] Szalai chose to act as buffer rather than a messenger. Burcham recalls, "My boss 'forgot' to tell me this until several years later."[22]

Burcham flew most of the Boeing 720 sims. What was the next step? Burcham needed to test the concept in actual flight. Thus, he needed a real airplane and a real pilot.

In March of 1990, Burcham paid a visit to the pilots' office. He ambled over to a pilot at his desk. He asked, "What do you think about using engine thrust for flight control? Would you like to take a look? How about flying a rough sim?" The pilot was Gordon Fullerton.

Fullerton was in his early fifties then, a graceful, athletic man with pale blue eyes that could gleam with humor. His face was burnished, even wizened perhaps from thousands of hours of flying in the fierce glare of the desert. Everyone on the base called him Gordo, this ex-astronaut and test pilot whose skills were the stuff of legend.

Fullerton's eyes glittered at Burcham's questions. Yes, he was definitely interested. Here was the man who had brought the STS 51F Space Shuttle down at Dryden willing to try to land a crippled commercial liner—or at least the simulation of one.

In an instant in the hallways at Dryden, PCA gained credibility.

It was some combination of curiosity and the challenge that hooked Fullerton. He followed Burcham to the plywood cockpit. Burcham mentioned that he himself, after some practice, had accomplished a successful landing using the throttles for control. "How would you like to try?" he asked.[23]

When Fullerton tried this unusual system, he entered a new realm. Where normal flight controls had done his bidding in an eyeblink, even in simulation the big lethargic engines might take what seemed like an eternity to respond. It was wait-and-see flying, a sort of dismaying process of anticipation, especially because the real-world situation would be one of desperation. The pilot commanded; the pilot waited. Later, one NASA test pilot referred to this type of flying as "herding a cow across the sky."[24]

---

[20] Kenneth J. Szalai, unpublished note, 14 Mar. 1990.

[21] Kenneth J. Szalai, interview with Dill Hunley, July 1998.

[22] Burcham, "Cleared for Landing," 21

[23] Burcham interview, 12 Aug. 1998.

[24] Purifoy interview.

To a nonpilot, the comparison would be driving on the freeway and having to turn the steering wheel nearly half a minute in advance of the vehicle's response. A phugoid cycle, for instance, lasts about 60 seconds and the thrust input to damp it must be given more than 20 seconds before there will be a perceptible indication that the input has had an effect. If the pilot gives a command, then observes no reaction, he may repeat the command and overcorrect with damaging effect. Without flight controls, if the airplane noses up, threatening to stall, the pilot will push his throttles forward, the reverse of the thrust input needed. In these last-resort circumstances, Joe Conley points out, "pilots will revert to natural instincts and natural flying instincts will kill you."[25]

Burcham's insight, which dated back to the sketch on the napkin, was that while a pilot would find it impossible to stop a phugoid with less than a 50/50 chance of even nudging the thrust in the right half of the oscillation, if a computer could help— if it could receive responses from motion sensors 40 times per second and react to each with a tiny correcting, nearly imperceptible nudge of the throttle—the airplane could be controlled.

Flying TOC (Throttles Only Control) was tough. But after five or six tries at the sim, Fullerton mastered the task. His technical curiosity may have weighed in as one factor, but the larger factor was the challenge. Ego in abundance is required of flyers in his occupation. Test and research pilots needed it to function, given the risks involved. The risks were real. If you look up at any street sign in the numerous roads intersecting around the Edwards runways, you see the names of pilots who have gone down in fireballs on the desert just beyond.

Fullerton had followed the Sioux City incident as closely as Burcham. As a research pilot who daily faced risk and the potential for deadly surprise, he admired what the pilots at Sioux City had accomplished. "What you guys did blew me away," he later told Dennis Fitch, the airline check pilot who had come forward that day from the passenger section to work the throttles.[26] In these early stages, Fullerton brought an additional front to the attack on the problem, one a bit ignored since then. He sought to develop a set of practical guidelines to help pilots whose airplanes lost some or all flight control surfaces.[27]

In addition to his willingness to evaluate sim flights, Fullerton made another contribution. He had noticed that some guest simulation pilots had problems even after the PCA was engaged. "One fighter test pilot," remembers a Dryden controls engineer, "never did get the hang of it."[28] At first glance, the stick had seemed the most efficient way to introduce and control PCA. But in a catastrophe, the pilot might expect the stick to respond immediately as in normal flight. Fullerton suggested putting the controls in thumbwheels, the hardware typically used in operating autopilots. Two thumbwheels were added to the panel, one for dialing in lateral commands, the other for longitudinal commands. Tests with more guest pilots confirmed the decision. "The thumbwheels," says Jim Stewart, "put it in the comfort zone."[29]

---

[25] Joseph Conley, telephone interview with author from NASA Ames, 19 June 1998.

[26] Dennis Fitch, telephone interview with author, 15 July 1998.

[27] Gordon Fullerton, interview with author, 7 July 1998.

[28] Burken interview.

[29] Stewart interview.

Another significant breakthrough came from Joe Conley. As he worked through landing data in analytics, he stepped back mentally and asked himself if there were some way to make his outcomes more predictable. Burcham had conjectured about using the ILS (Instrument Landing System)—a radio-beamed tracking system that helps guide actual airplanes onto the runway in bad weather. What if the inputs from ILS were added to the inputs PCA used? Conley designed a simple ILS and added it to the PCA sim. It was a deft move. In terms of the sim, the scheme was merely a pleasant improvement, but in a year, in terms of real airplanes coming down onto the runway, it played an important role.

Some PCA skeptics viewed Sioux City as a once-only instance. "Why bother?" they explained, "because it will never happen again." Burcham and Fullerton did some research looking for other airplane accidents that could be traced to lost hydraulic controls. At first, the naysayers were confirmed—nothing showed up. Then one afternoon while traveling, Jim Stewart gave a talk about PCA. Afterwards, an Air Force man came up to him out of the audience. "I have to talk to you," he said.[30]

In 1975, an incident happened in Vietnam to a USAF C-5 transport evacuating orphans from Saigon. When a bulkhead failed in the aft fuselage, all hydraulics to the tail were lost. The pilots had flight controls for roll but none for pitch. They tried using the throttle and found that it provided some pitch control, but were unable to control a phugoid on approach for emergency landing. The phugoid caused the aircraft to crash-land into a rice paddy. Of 314 passengers, 138 died but 176 survived.

In the months that followed, the Dryden searchers discovered other incidents. In 1985, a Japan Airlines flight suffered total hydraulic loss. Out of control, the airplane flew for 30 minutes before hitting a mountain, killing 520 people. The same year as the Sioux City crash, a Navy fighter flying over Jasper County, Indiana, lost hydraulic controls, and when the aircraft rolled off uncontrollably to the right at an angle of 90 degrees, the pilot ejected. Another crew on a commercial flight near San Diego found the airplane about to stall in an uncontrollable pitch-up when they used throttle controls, changed pitch by thrust modulation, and landed safely. A 1974 flight departing Paris was less fortunate. The airliner lost some flight controls, diving into the ground at high speed. All 346 aboard perished.

It was grim arithmetic but was part of the factoring needed to convince an industry and its regulators to look seriously at PCA. As other accidents came to light, the Dryden researchers assembled a list of relatively recent incidents involving more than 1,100 fatalities.[31]

* * *

One of the guest pilots in the spring of 1991 was Al Haynes, captain of the Sioux City Flight 232. During the year after the crash, he began to give an inspirational

[30] Stewart interview.

[31] Cf. Frank W. Burcham et al., *Development and Flight Evaluation of an Emergency Digital Flight Control System Using Only Engine Thrust on an F-15 Airplane* (Edwards, CA: NASA TP 3627, 1996): 2-5, and Military Airlift Command History Office, *Anything, Anywhere, Anytime: An Illustrated History of the Military Airlift Command, 1941-1991* (Scott Air Force Base, IL: HQ MAC, 1991), pp. 152-153.

speech around the country regarding cockpit resource management and emergency preparedness. He came to Dryden and spoke to an overflow audience.[32] Afterwards Burcham and Fullerton took him to see the 720 sim, but when they invited him to fly it, he turned them down.

Here was unexpected resistance. This pilot had been rock-steady during his ordeal. In audiotapes of his remarks to the Sioux Gateway control tower, there was not a crack in his voice as Haynes announced as casually as if he were talking about weekend recreation plans, "We're not gonna make the runway, fellas."[33]

But this was different. He hesitated; perhaps his eyes moistened.

"I don't think I want to fly the simulation."

"Why?" asked Fullerton.

"I don't know . . . to get back in a cockpit faced with the same situation."

He stared a moment at the dim contraption. But he did get in; he flew the sim later that afternoon. He punched the PCA button, approached the runway; PCA eased him to glideslope, and the gray runway on the video screen came closer. On his first effort he was able to put the plane safely on the ground.

Al Haynes was pleased.[34]

Figure 8. Al Haynes in the Boeing 720 simulator with (left to right) Gordon Fullerton, Bill Burcham, and Jim Stewart. (NASA photo EC91-316-2 by Bob Brown).

---

[32] Al Haynes, interview by telephone with author, 16 June 1998.

[33] Al Haynes, from video accompanying speech, "The Crash of Flgt. 232," 24 May 1991.

[34] Most of the Haynes and simulator story come from the Gordon Fullerton interview.

* * *

Burcham's idea *was* big. It was big in the unexpected ways it kicked in sometimes more strongly than the engineers had ever predicted. Bill was the first impetus behind the project, but PCA was much bigger than any one individual, and teams would form and reform, members dropping in and out, one person making some significant, defining contribution, then another. At the NASA center best known for supersonics, this subsonic idea lumbered along with the speed of a transport. It survived, moving through an institution, through units and sub-units, a bit of a stealth project because it had no budget to be shot down, moving through "mature technology," moving through an engineer's off-time on Saturday afternoon, through carpool debates, reviews, briefings. And PCA was about to reconfigure with another unit that would help it survive, the U.S. Air Force.

Burcham was looking for funds. He could not "buy" an airplane, but he needed to buy a feasibility study, to look at how to prove the PCA concept, how to reconfigure a real airplane with this technology. The Air Force's Terry Neighbor from Wright-Patterson Air Force Base, who headed a group investigating controls integration, had listened to Burcham pitch PCA to another Air Force unit, which ultimately expressed lack of interest. Neighbor did find PCA interesting. He recalls it as "another dimension of something we were doing." Neighbor went back to his office, got his hands on some managerial discretionary funds, initially $100,000, which in the scheme of more visible projects was pocket change, but which for PCA was a vital infusion,

the funds needed for a feasibility study on the project's first real airplane testbed, an F-15.[35]

NASA Dryden had an F-15 in the hangar at Edwards. The F-15 is a high-performance fighter airplane from McDonnell Douglas Aerospace.[36] What attracted Burcham was that this Dryden F-15 had two computer systems, a digital flight control computer, FCC, and digital electronic engine controls, DEEC. These two systems can "talk" to each other, and both are programmable. Earlier projects— most recently, HIDEC—had already loaded Dryden's F-15 with expensive testing instrumentation. Despite these attractions, among all the airplanes in the world if the researchers had been given a choice, the F-15 would have ranked among the last.

The problem was the engines. They were two big, powerful turbofans relegated to the rear of the airframe. A mere 12 inches separated the two brutes, and if PCA technology depended on differential thrust between the right and left engines, how would the F-15 respond? Some rough sims had looked encouraging, but sims were sims, and the robust power of flight control surfaces might have masked the effects of the closely spaced engines.

The study was contracted to McDonnell Douglas Aerospace in St. Louis, Missouri. New faces now appeared on the team. McDonnell's Jim Urnes became project manager for the task and Ed Wells was design and flight test engineer. Now trips to simulators took Burcham and his colleagues to the spectacular F-15 simulation in St. Louis. It was a real F-15 cockpit with real F-15 controls, and

---

[35] Terry Neighbor, interview by telephone with author, 4 Aug. 1998.

[36] Today, the companies mentioned in this history are all part of Boeing. But in these pages, they will be designated as they were then separately known for most of the duration of the PCA work. They included McDonnell Douglas Aerospace in St. Louis, which did PCA studies for the F-15; McDonnell Douglas Aerospace Long Beach, which did PCA studies for the MD-11; and Douglas Aircraft Company operating the MD-11 out of Long Beach and testing in Yuma. Boeing was a separate and independent company headquartered in Seattle.

dramatic scenery wrap-around on the inside of a 40-foot dome. If Burcham had an hour remaining at the end of a day devoted to the big HIDEC project, he ran a PCA test.

Safety features designed into the sim were the ones to be designed into the real airplane. All modifications were software ones—with one exception, the addition of a cockpit controller for PCA. The hydraulics were never turned off. The pilot used the emergency mode of the mechanical flight control system, which did not have the flight control computers automatically driving the control surfaces. At the slightest touch to stick or rudder pedals, the pilot could engage the normal flight control surfaces.

Dryden's Tom Wolf introduced many modifications to the Dryden F-15 sim to account for the new F-15 configuration. Ed Wells, the St. Louis F-15 specialist, added these control laws to the McDonnell sim and customized the 720 version of the flight control laws for the F-15.

Hardware arose as an issue. Fullerton had voted for thumbwheels as the controllers of choice, but McDonnell decided the question needed systematic review. And the thumbwheels posed a problem: McDonnell had a thumbwheel panel from an F-4 Control Configured Vehicle (CCV) program that was qualified only for lab use. The researchers did not have a flight-qualified unit to install in a real airplane. Jury-rigging knobs for a sim was one thing but installing hardware not certified for flight was another. "Our shoestring program did not have the funding for designing or building new ones," remembers Burcham. McDonnell framed four options for the study. These included the central control stick, a ministick spring-loaded and moved by force, another spring-loaded ministick moved by degrees, and the F-4 CCV thumbwheels. Each option had negatives, and a series of guest pilots flying the sim again decisively confirmed the wisdom of the thumbwheels.[37]

Where to get the flight hardware? At this point, the Air Force came to the rescue,

Figure 9. Gordon Fullerton and the two "brutes" (engines) in the F-15 after he had landed the aircraft using only engine power for control on 21 April 1993. (NASA photo EC93-41034-3 by Larry Sammons).

[37] Burcham interview, 17 June 1998; Edward Wells and James Urnes, *Design and Flight Test of the Propulsion Controlled Aircraft (PCA) Flight Control System on the NASA F-15 Test Aircraft* (Edwards, CA: NASA CR 186028, Feb. 1994): 9-11.

and Major Bob Yeager, who had joined the PCA team, tracked down the thumbwheels still in an F-4 CCV resting in a flight museum in Dayton, Ohio. He talked the museum into loaning the thumbwheel panel; herded the curious transaction through stacks of paper regulations; and for the life of the project, the F-15 sported flight-qualified thumbwheels.

It was clear from the beginning that the team would need to perform actual flight tests of PCA. Some engineers say that flight tests are not needed when a good simulation will suffice. But PCA itself was so new, so different, that many questions arose. The test to provide answers to these questions would take place up in the air.[38]

The first dedicated throttles-only control flight test arrived the morning of 2 July 1991. In the summer, Dryden flight research often starts at the crack of dawn before the thermals produce strong updrafts. Sometimes the hangar crew begins as early as 2 a.m. These moments have a curious look—the operations area is a world of metal and certainties but at that sleepy hour displays all pastel colors, the desert sky before sunrise, a pale Easter-egg blue, and the airplane glim-

mering softly like a reflection. Fullerton strolled out to the F-15 with his test cards clipped to his sleeve, ready to take this project to the next stage. But although the team had anticipated some problems, although they had replaced one engine with an identical mate to the other, they were not prepared for what happened next.

The flight did not go as planned. Fullerton took off in the sleek fighter and then brought the F-15 up to altitude to begin following his test cards. He set up the airplane for TOC and in the instant joined the brotherhood of Haynes and Fitch at Sioux City: no ailerons to control airplane roll; no elevator to dictate pitch; no rudder to yaw a turn at command.

All Fullerton had was his hand on the throttles and even before he moved them, strange things began to happen. "I was looking at the sky and then the dirt and all over,"[39] he remarked. When he tried a gentle pressure to correct pitch, the airplane entered a roll. He reacted. He throttled to stop the roll. The F-15 re- sponded by pitching down, then up, seemingly with a mind of its own.

What had happened? In mid-air, in an instant, Fullerton guessed at a part of the

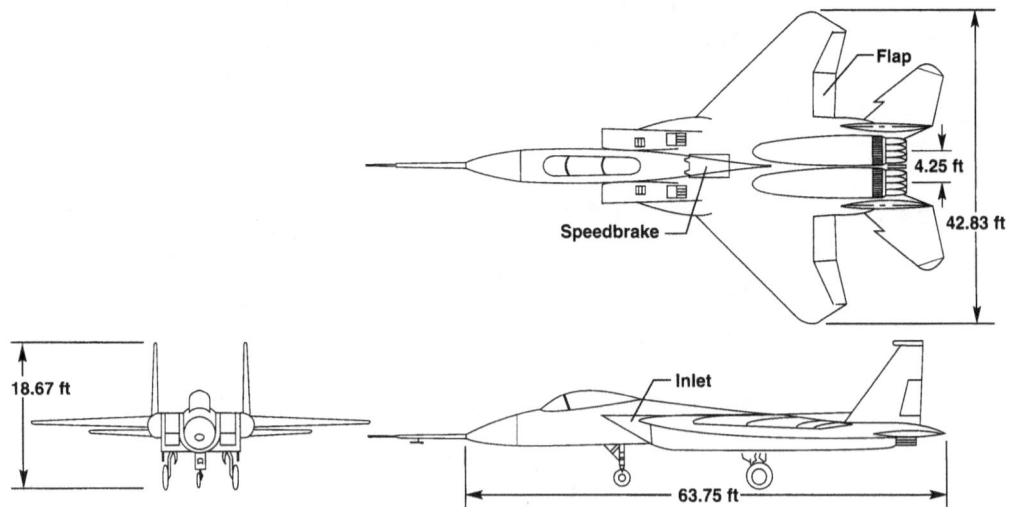

Figure 10. Three- view drawing of an F-15 airplane.

---

[38] Fullerton interview.

[39] Gordon Fullerton, from transcript of interview with Lane Wallace, 7 Sept. 1995.

answer. In the simulation, the mathematical model had provided him with two perfectly identical engines. But they were just models. Even "identical" engines had slight differences. When control surfaces operated, these minimal differences had no effect. They were masked by the power of the flight controls. But when you turned the normal controls off, the big engines, with a little nudge, did big deeds. Because one engine spooled up to full throttle sooner than the other, every input sent the F-15 careening across the sky.[40]

When Fullerton brought the airplane down the glideslope to the runway, he did so with normal flight controls turned on and at the moment of touchdown, the one proof of the day might have seemed to be: you can never land an F-15 airplane safely using throttles-only control. The faces above in the control room had a

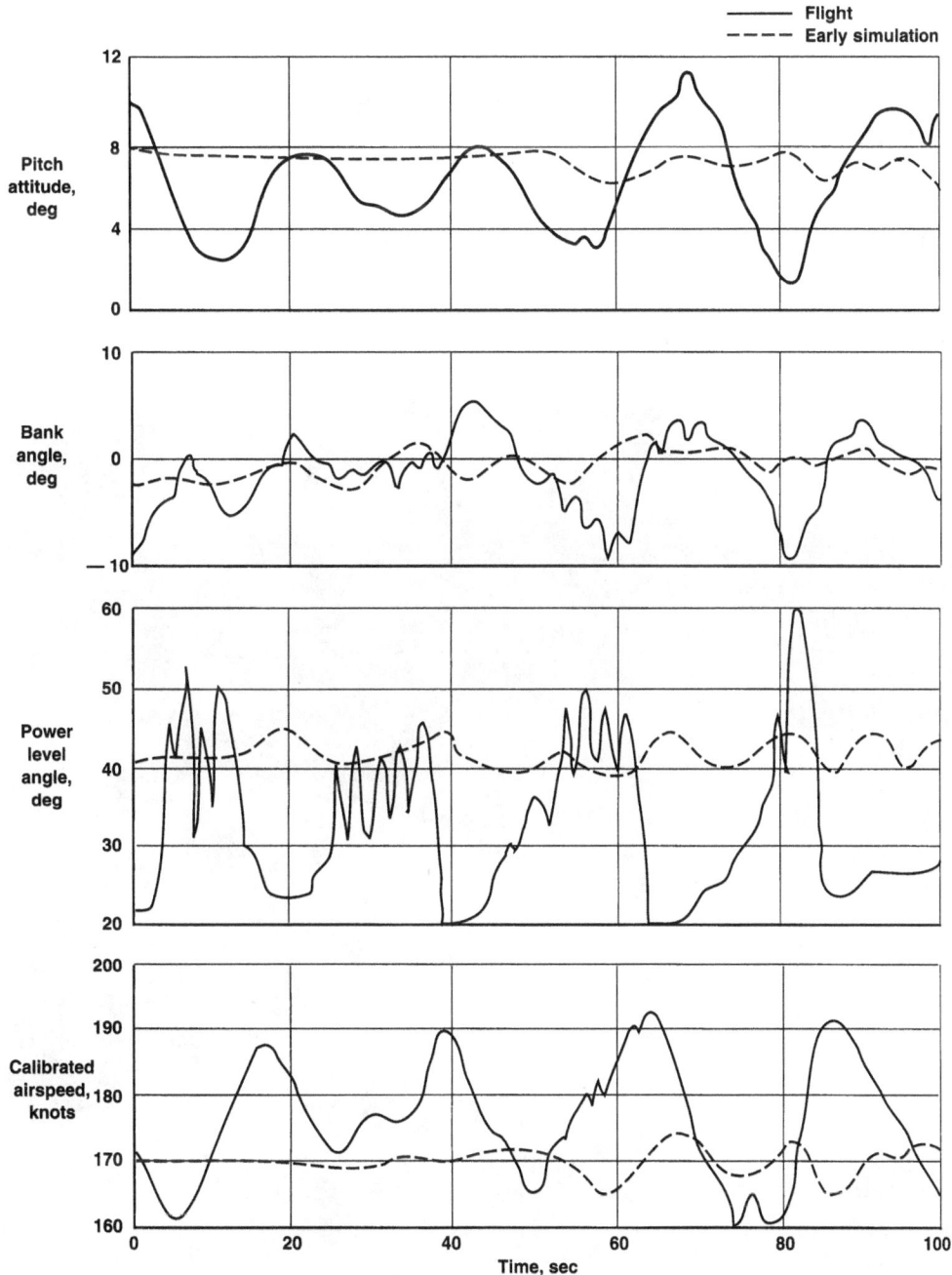

Figure 11. Diagrams showing the early F-15 simulation versus actual flight in the F-15 in manual, throttles-only approaches at 170 knots with the flaps up and the control augmentation system off.

[40] Fullerton interview.

stricken look. And surely in the hallways, the naysayers were nodding 'I-told-you-so.'

"Humbling" is the word Fullerton uses in summation; "it's a matter of pride. I can do anything. This airplane's not going to get the best of me. And it did. It really did."[41] When the F-15's flight controls were turned off, the airplane became aerodynamically very unstable, what Fullerton called a "squirrelly airplane." As far as his colleagues could tell, Burcham appeared unfazed. But he trudged to his car with a stack of test data printouts, and it was only Tuesday night. Usually, he waited until Friday night to bring them home. He would have the long drive across the bleak desert to ask himself questions. Why was the F-15 sim so different from the real airplane? As one associate said, "When Bill started to deal with these propulsion effects and effects

near landing, there weren't any guidelines to help him . . . he was going to have to write the book."[42]

* * *

The team set about making major modifications to the F-15 sim. If the sim was improved, they should be able to duplicate what Fullerton had seen in actual flight. In the first days, they realized that the F-15's center of gravity (CG) shifted as the fuel was consumed, and the airplane's weight and weight distribution changed. They modeled the sim to incorporate this data. The F-15 went to a second flight test, but the results remained poor. Fullerton could maneuver somewhat up and away, but the F-15 without control surfaces was an unstable airplane. He did not have anywhere near enough control for a safe landing. When he pushed the collective throttles up, the airplane rolled.

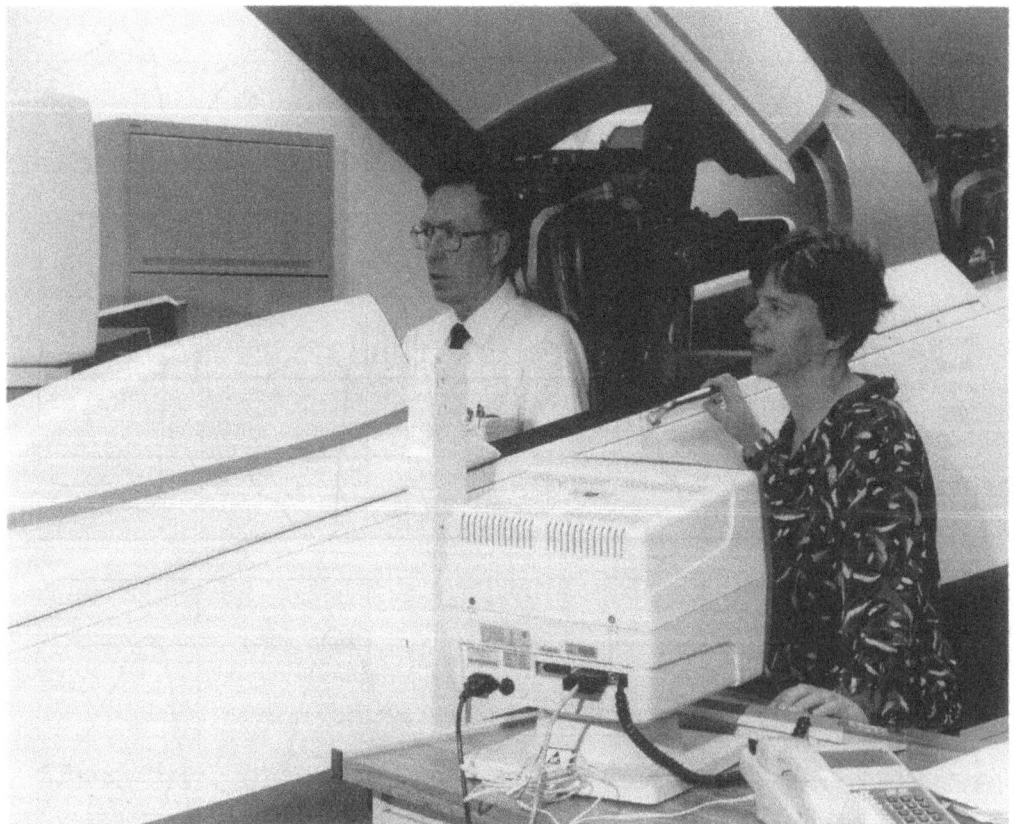

Figure 12. Bill Burcham and Trindel Maine at an F-15 simulator session. (NASA photo EC95-43026-2 by Jim Ross).

---

[41] Fullerton interview with Lane Wallace.

[42] Burken interview.

A series of tests followed, flights, sims. Some of this process was "tweaking" and "de-bugging." The team had larger, shadowy factors to discover, and one of them turned out to be inlet effects.

Trindel Maine, a Dryden engineer who joined the team at this stage and had a reputation as a wizard at scanning data sheets and spotting a trend, saw the process for what it was. A daunting number of factors come into play when an airplane maneuvers with throttles, and the researcher at last brought this one to light. The big, overhanging ramp-air inlets are beside the pilot. It turned out that when Fullerton wanted the nose to drop and pulled the throttles back, the reduced airflow to the engines pushed up on the inlet ramps and raised the nose. This effect is normally masked by the pilot's commanding a minor change in the elevator position, but with no elevator movement, the inlet effect caused the airplane briefly to pitch in the wrong direction. The Dryden and McDonnell team developed a model of the inlet effect and added it to their simulations at Edwards and St. Louis. Now the TOC in

the F-15 sim went up a notch in difficulty but still did not match the flight research data.

Another problem involved the ground effects. "Ground effects is a black art," says Trindel Maine; "we just don't have any good ground effects models out there."[43] Some ground effects studies do exist, but they are based on fixed throttle settings and are not well modeled. Normal flight controls operate so powerfully, they mask ground effects. When the F-15 came within a wingspan of touchdown, it entered this realm of unruly aerodynamics.

The engineers needed ground-effects data that were non-existent. "This was an area where the simulator model was suspect . . . where we were quite concerned about knowing what we'd be dealing with," explains Maine. The team commissioned a study addressing ground effects on F-15 landings.[44] The study was conducted in the traditional fixed-throttle setting and, as a consequence, did not match very well what the team encountered afterwards in PCA flight. "The final answer didn't become clear until much later," Maine

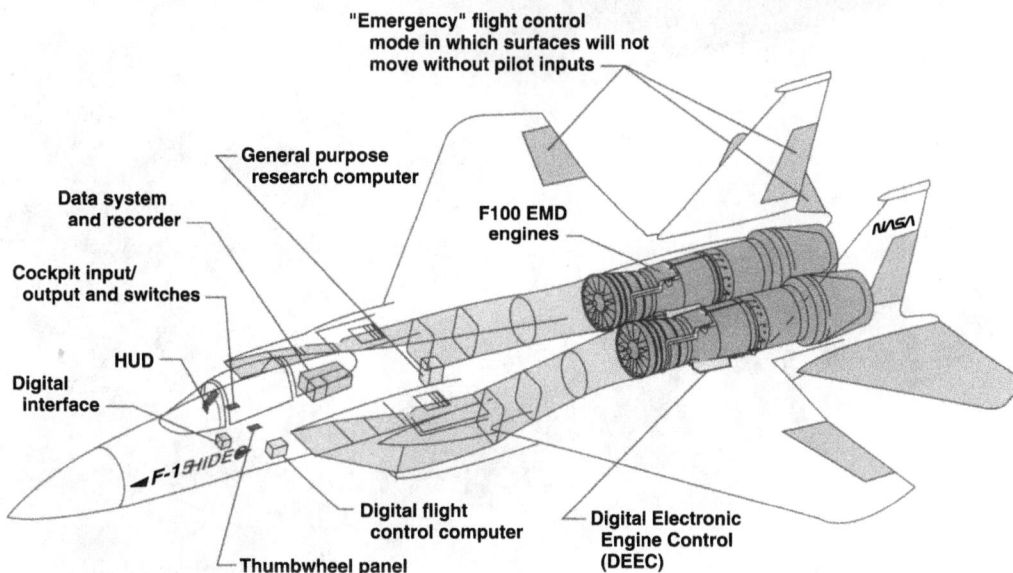

Figure 13. Features of the PCA system on the NASA F-15 HIDEC airplane.

---

[43] Trindel Maine, interview with author, 2 July 1998.

[44] See Stephen Corda et al., *Dynamic Ground Effects Flight of an F-15 Aircraft* (Edwards, CA: NASA TM 460, June 1994).

remarked; ". . . the PCA control laws moving the throttle actively during the landing phase had a big impact on how the ground effects actually affected the flight path." As it learned more about ground effects, the team worked to minimize the most severe effect, an alarmingly high sink rate just before touchdown.[45]

In addition, the engineers modeled the sims more closely to the Pratt & Whitney engines, identifying lags and rate limits. They put modeling in the sim for landing gear and its actual effects on aerodynamics. Gyroscopic movements from the powerful engines were factored in. But despite all these efforts, flight difficulties persisted.

"Some unmodeled effect was obviously present," said Burcham. The team had not solved this mystery, but it hoped that the computer and the feedback sensors of the PCA system would be able to accommodate the problem. "It was time to see," said Burcham, "if the PCA system—with the computer taking the pilot inputs, factoring in the sensor feedbacks, and figuring out where to put the throttles—would work."[46]

In the early weeks of 1993, Fullerton conducted the initial flights with the PCA system engaged. PCA showed much improvement over TOC, but still presented some problems. The noisy signals from some of the sensors required filtering, and bank angle feedback was needed. Fortunately, back in an earlier design review,

Figure 14. Gordon Fullerton climbing aboard the F-15 for the 21 April 1993 research flight. (NASA photo EC93-41034-4 by Larry Sammons).

---

[45] Maine interview.

[46] His comment on a draft of this narrative.

Glenn Gilyard had noticed that the bank angle was not one of the feedback sensors and had it added. Ed Wells had introduced flexibility into the test process by making available points in the software where the pilot could select variable gains, filters, multipliers, and gain schedules. It provided a quantum leap. The researchers could carry on real-time dialogue over the radio with the pilot and alter PCA. It was working fast—it was depending on a small team of highly skilled individuals.[47]

With the changes, the team improved control enough to try low approaches to the runway.

Many standards apply to landing an airplane. Some resolve to this question during a commercial aircraft landing: would your coffee stay in its cup (assuming the flight attendants had not collected cups before landing, as they normally do)? But others resolve differently: do you walk away with your life? PCA is

Figure 15. Gordon Fullerton and Bill Burcham next to the F-15 aircraft. (NASA photo EC93-41034-11 by Jim Ross).

[47] Jim Urnes, interview by telephone with author, 26 June 1998.

Figure 16. Three-
view drawing of the
McDonnell Douglas
MD-11 research
airplane.

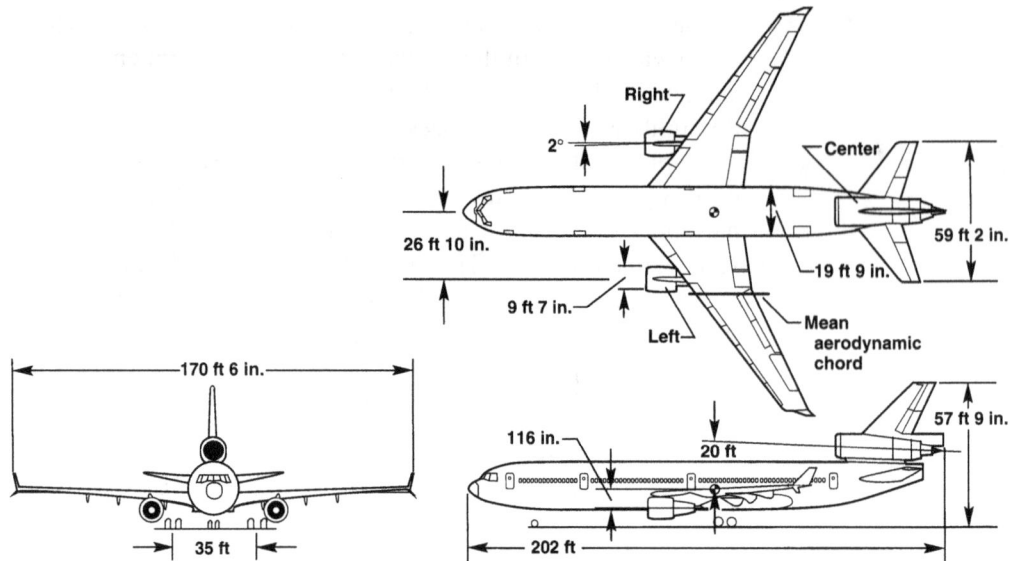

Right

2°

Center

26 ft 10 in.

59 ft 2 in.

9 ft 7 in.

19 ft 9 in.

Left

Mean
aerodynamic
chord

170 ft 6 in.

57 ft 9 in.

116 in.

20 ft

35 ft

202 ft

defined by catastrophic alternative. In fact, later, PCA had the robustness to make landings so smooth they were difficult to distinguish from normal ones.

On the morning of 21 April 1993, however, when Gordon Fullerton flew the F-15 on the downwind approach to Edwards' runway, he did not have the word "gentle" in his pilot cards. He used the PCA system for a series of approaches at altitude at different trim speeds, and then he brought the F-15 down near ground level. "When we flew within 10 feet, we knew we had success," recalls Jim Urnes, the McDonnell project manager.[48]

On the next flight, Fullerton made aeronautics history when he flew the first PCA landing. He descended in a very shallow approach to 20 feet above the ground; then his sink rate rose quickly to 8 feet per second. The unfazed Fullerton, however, remained confident and brought the F-15 to a "firm but acceptable" touchdown 6 feet left of the runway centerline. "Smoke flew off the tires,"

remembers Urnes.[49] Nevertheless, the system had landed an airplane.

The system might not pass the coffee-cup test. But it could get you safely down.

"It was like landing on the moon," recalls one project manager about the applause for the F-15 landing that erupted in the Dryden control room and echoed around the industry for weeks to come. "Look Ma No Hands" trumpeted *Aviation Week & Space Technology*.[50]

In a real disaster, PCA would be the technology of last resort for first-time users. The team addressed this issue after the F-15 landings, when it invited six pilots unfamiliar with PCA to test approaches and go-rounds. All the pilots flew the system successfully and were enthusiastic about PCA's capabilities. "Pitch control was awesome," said Navy Lieutenant Len Hamilton. He indicated that he would rather have PCA than the backup control technology in his current F-14.[51]

[48] Urnes interview.

[49] *Ibid.*

[50] See Michael Dornheim, "Industry Outlook: Look Ma, No Hands," *Aviation Week & Space Technology* (3 May 1995): 11.

[51] See Appendix D for guest pilot remarks at greater length.

The engineers, pilots, managers, all of them had understood one brutal point about the industry position: until you proved this technology on a small airplane, you had no chance of getting on a big airplane. Now that they had proved it on the F-15, the next airplane waiting for PCA was the MD-11.

The MD-11 is a widebody transport airplane that succeeded the earlier DC-10, a huge three-engine vehicle more than two-thirds of a football field in length. The MD-11 with its full flight control autoland system, its digitally controlled engines, and fully integrated design was a next-generation aircraft, the type of aircraft that was in the cards from the day the idea was sketched on the napkin.

Even before the historic PCA landing of the F-15, efforts were made to arrange PCA experiments on a large transport airplane. One crucial moment occurred during a meeting at NASA Headquarters in Washington, D.C.

In December 1992, Dwain Deets, then Acting Director of Dryden Research Engineering, attended this pivotal Headquarters session. Assembling around the conference table were executives from every big player in aircraft manufacturing and also the directors from the other NASA centers. Bob Whitehead, Director of Subsonic Transportation in the Office of Aeronautics and Space Technology at Headquarters, convened the group. Szalai had asked Deets to attend and represent him, and Burcham attended as technical support.

Deets had spent many years as a Dryden spokesperson in Washington, D.C., meetings. He recalls a sense that day of venturing into hostile territory. The issue was endorsement. Whitehead would not let the centers proceed on a project unless they had industry endorsement. From the start, Boeing had been very cool to the idea of PCA. Whitehead was not looking for mere industry neutrality. "Whatever it is we do," he was quoted as saying, "it's got to buy its way onto the airplane." Another concern for Deets was NASA Langley, the center that specializes in subsonics. Burcham and his colleagues were venturing on Langley turf. Burcham had already briefed Langley about PCA and had not been well received. In the future of this technology, there would arise remarkable cooperation between Langley and Dryden. But at that time, observers recall, jealousy was often the norm between centers. And it did not help that a series of recent promotions to Headquarters had gone to Langley execs, many of them advisors to Whitehead.

Whitehead, however, when he opened the meeting spoke favorably about PCA. He was brief; he did not cajole, debate, or insist; and Deets had the distinct sense of watching a referee toss a ball into play at the start of a contest. When his turn came, Deets gave the briefest of presentations—everyone at the table knew what the issue was. Next, the floor moved around the table from one executive to another. John King, from McDonnell Douglas Aerospace in Long Beach, gave an extremely strong endorsement. So did NTSB member John Lauber. Finally, came the turn for the man from Boeing.

"I never saw anything like it," Deets remembers today with a touch of wonderment. "He didn't say anything. Everyone at the table had their eyes fixed on him. It all hinged on this moment. But he didn't say a word; he just glared down for quite some time, the room utterly silent, and then he made a quick movement; he made this thumbs-up sign. That was all, that was that . . . it was a done deal."

The meeting moved quickly to other items on its agenda. When Deets and Burcham returned to Dryden, they brought home good news.

"It's a go," they said.[52]

---

[52] Dwain Deets, interview with author, 1 July 1998.

The MD-11 experiment was destined to be much more successful than the F-15. But the crises to be faced were different and these had nothing to do with harrowing test flights. The crises occurred in well-cushioned conference rooms. Now the project had a $2.5 million budget line per year resulting from the advisory meeting in Washington. Now there were contracts, subcontracts, and work orders rather than reliance on the good nature of an engineer at the end of a long day. And there was the assignment of a project manager from NASA Dryden, first Russ Barber, then Bob Baron, and finally Joel Sitz ably guiding the project through NASA internal processes. Dryden engineers now included Trindel Maine, John Burken, and Burcham, and meanwhile Fullerton invited another NASA pilot, Dana Purifoy, to join in the flight research. New faces appeared because McDonnell Douglas Aerospace in St. Louis had developed the F-15, but the Douglas Aircraft unit in Long Beach and Yuma had the MD-11 under active development. The project assembled talented test pilots John Miller and Ralph Luczak as well as Walt Smith for simulation studies. The remarkably ingenious engineer Jeff Kahler was sent by Honeywell to install the PCA software in the flight control computer it had manufactured. During these early days, GE and Pratt & Whitney, manufacturers of engines slung on MD-11s, sent engineers to the meetings. It was anyone's guess what engines would be attached when they at last found their specific testbed.

The MD-11 sims developed nicely. "You sure you guys turned the button off?" asked one guest pilot, a comment that was repeated for months. But although flight controls were turned off and PCA engaged, something else subtly was turned off. Months passed; an inertia began developing. One resident expert from McDonnell admitted off the record, "This scared me to turn off all the traditional flight controls."

Burcham had shepherded the PCA into a new environment. At his own desert lab, debate had been informal, personal, and in-your-face. Douglas Aircraft was corporate, pleasant, and polite. A subtle transition had been made—he was no longer an associate but a client.

"The project had some difficulty," remembers Russ Barber, "in transitioning from sim studies to airplane modifications and operations. We kept going down to Long Beach for reviews and we kept getting more and more sims."[53] Burcham does not like to talk about the period.

What was the problem? It was, in the end, economics. None of the commercial airline manufacturers will specify a sticker price on their wares. But when you see a jumbo jetliner on the runway, you may be looking at as much as 150 million dollars. Who would lightly take such an expensive product and, in terms of safe flight, go backwards? Who would risk it? Burcham had at last gotten a budget for PCA, but within the parameters of the industry, he was still on a shoestring.

Although Douglas produced MD-11s, it did not own a single one. The firm did not keep its 150-million-dollar product on the shelf as if it were retail. The issue became: could Burcham get an airplane?

Burcham himself had worn the project manager hat whenever needed; his new Long Beach technical associate, John Feather, played that role now in a part-time capacity. In addition to engineering duties, Feather filed applications and attended reviews in efforts to find a real airplane. But all negotiations proved fruitless. At this low point, even as Burcham spent hours on the phone, in his phrase "going round and round," he at last talked Douglas Aircraft into appointing a full-time project manager. The man appointed was Drew Pappas.[54]

---

[53] Marvin R. Barber, interview with author, 18 June 1998.

[54] Frank W. Burcham, interview with author, 17 June 1998.

"When Drew came on," recalls Russ Barber about the first week in June, 1994, "almost overnight it turned around."[55] Pappas is a short balding man with a dark mustache who insists on modesty. "I was along to carry the bags," he says. But as many elements fell into place at his touch, it became clear Pappas knew Douglas Aircraft very well. He knew how things got done, where the procedural gears turned, how to keep the regulatory process from jamming. "I have a Mr. Fix-It mind," he grins. "When I don't know what to do, I try to get the answer and fix it." He dismisses what he does as "mother-henning," and he sees himself as a professional worrier, the detail-cruncher along for the ride with genius.[56] Within a relatively short time, he found them an airplane, the testbed, the MD-11. He mother-henned a 150-million-dollar airplane onto the runway.

The project regained momentum, confidence returned, but a surprise awaited Pappas. Doubts about PCA still troubled some of the most distinguished members of his team. One afternoon at a simulation in Long Beach, two colleagues spoke up. These men had flown TOC and knew it was rough. They anticipated two problem areas: the degree of complexity in the landing and the design of software to handle the challenge of actual flight. PCA technology might never work, they warned.

Pappas recalls driving home stunned afterwards. Now the questions whirled in his mind. The implications began to settle in. He wondered if the doubts voiced by his team members would become a "self-fulfilling prophecy." He hesitated before a step both unpleasant and risky. "What if I requested changes in personnel?" he asked himself. "Are these guys going to kill my project, or worse, are they right?"

By the time Pappas pulled in the driveway at home, he had reached a decision. He would request no roster changes; he would re-focus his own horizons. "My objective," he explains, "was not to achieve success, but to determine if the task was feasible."[57]

Flight 232 pilot Al Haynes had raised an issue after he enthused about PCA. How do you reduce the speed of the airplane? During this stage, the engineers found the answers always proved specific to the airplane. Some airplanes have electronically-commanded stabilizers which, even with hydraulics failed, will reduce speed. Others have electrically or pneumatically operated flaps that drop and reduce speed. Moving the center of gravity to the rear of the airplane can also reduce speed. Lowering the landing gear slows the airplane—the open wheel wells and hinged landing gear doors produce drag. Many factors were found to influence airplane speed.

Douglas Aircraft introduced numerous safety checks and procedures into these experiments. In fact, at first only one engine flew PCA in actual flight. But on the historic date of 27 August 1995, when Flight 221 went up over Yuma with both engines PCA-equipped, the system once again showed its surprising capability.[58]

The pilots took the airplane to 10,000 feet altitude and turned the PCA system on. It performed as smoothly as a normal

---

[55] Barber interview.

[56] Drew Pappas, interview by telephone with author, 17 July 1998.

[57] Pappas interview.

[58] The designation "Flight 221" does not refer to the number of research flights in the PCA program. Rather, the number designates the flight in the total series of test flights performed by the specific MD-11 on any number of projects.

autopilot, holding the wings level, controlling flightpath to a few tenths of a degree, maintaining altitude to within plus or minus 20 feet. As his eyes moved over the panel in the cockpit, safety pilot John Miller became a convert. "On the first attempt, I understood the capability of the engineering team, and they had done a fantastic job."[59] Miller proved a powerful advocate for the most compelling proof, a real MD-11 touchdown, and it was Miller who begged landings and other test envelope expansions from Douglas management.

over the desert mountains." With the modified software installed, the engineering crew and pilots flew north that morning. Their destination was Edwards Air Force Base, with its vast natural landing site adjacent to Dryden and the main runway at Edwards where they would land. It was home in a sense, marginally more forgiving than Yuma in thermal intensity, and definitely friendlier in the length and width of its runways. At Edwards, Fullerton completed successful approaches to 100 feet, 50 feet, and 10 feet above the runway. As he

Figure 17. Pilot views of MD-11 performing a PCA Instrument Landing System-coupled approach and landing.

Figure 18. MD-11 touching down for the first time under engine power only, 11:38 a.m. August 29, 1995, at Edwards. (NASA photo EC95 43247-4 by Dennis Taylor).

As the MD-11 tests had moved to lower altitudes that August, the thermals—updrafts off the blazing Arizona sands—had begun to pose a significant challenge, especially in the afternoons when temperatures soared to 115 degrees. Kahler and Burken had worked feverishly to develop control law changes to improve PCA's tolerance to gusts and thermals.

On 29 August 1995, the MD-11 made its first PCA touchdown. The day started early at the Douglas airfield in Yuma. "The crew brief was at 4:30 a.m. in Yuma," recalls Burcham, "with takeoff just as the sun rose

finally approached for actual landing, the thermals began to buffet the airplane, yet, Burcham recalls, "Fullerton's approach looked good." The pilot left the flightpath command at -2 degrees, working the heading knob. At 100 feet he made the flightpath shallower, and the airplane came down smoothly at a sink rate of 4 feet per second on the centerline. Here was all the promise of the F-15 flights delivered home now in the landing of a commercial airliner. The videotape records it: the vast bird descending with all control surfaces motionless, an exhilarating but eerie sight.[60]

---

[59] John Miller, interview by telephone with author, 19 June 1998.

[60] Based on a description of the landing written by Frank W. Burcham on the original draft of this account.

On 29-30 November 1995, landings at Edwards demonstrated an improvement dating back to Joe Conley's inspiration, the addition of ILS coupling to PCA's arsenal of signals. Kahler connected the PCA and ILS software in the Honeywell computer on the MD-11. The result brought improved control to PCA and did not require additional emergency-procedure training for pilots. Kahler also added an autoflare to PCA's arsenal for these two landings, an improvement that demonstrated a feasible step toward "hands-off" emergency touchdowns.

In the fall of 1995, two dozen guest pilots from the major powers in commercial aviation were given the opportunity to operate PCA on the MD-11, flying an ILS-coupled landing to 100 AGL (100 feet above ground level) before initiating go-round.[61] The pilot comment cards

Figure 19. Research pilot Gordon Fullerton, project engineer Bill Burcham, control engineer John Burken, McDonnell Douglas' John Feather, and McDonnell Douglas project engineer Drew Pappas emerging from the MD-11 at the NASA Dryden ramp after the first PCA landing in the MD-11. (NASA photo EC95 432351-3 by Tony Landis).

[61] See Appendix F for remarks from the two-day guest pilot session.

thundered with wonder and praise, but beyond the hurrahs from demonstration and experiments was another experiment sometimes overlooked.

* * *

The ultimate test for PCA would be to turn off all the hydraulics. The flight tests had locked down all the surfaces, the ailerons, the rudder, the flaps, but in a real catastrophe, the surfaces would *float* to some position. Would it be a good position or a bad one? The sims had made predictions, forecasting a rather benign pitchover to a higher trim speed. The truth was uncertain. To turn off all hydraulics might start a deadly scenario. What was the worst that could happen? The result might be what the engineers call a "hardover," a dramatically asymmetric position, and because the ailerons creating it have a more powerful effect than engine controls, the engines could not power the MD-11 out of it.

Burcham saw it as a crux issue. John Miller brought something close to the physical courage he used in test piloting to the task of pleading this case. To the shock of all involved, he convinced management. Douglas gave them the go-ahead.

It was to be an ultimate test at the human level, too. On MD-11 flights, the engineers traveled at the rear of the airplane, sharing the risk that typically pilots faced alone. Observers at Douglas still speak with awe about the engineering team that pored over test displays and made significant changes in flight to gains and lags via intercom conversation with the pilot. Some projects might take three weeks to arrive at the same results. Some engineers might spend whole careers working on projects that never took them outside the laboratory.

"It was a bit eerie," recalls Joel Sitz, Dryden project manager when he remembers the change from dealing with PCA as paper and reports to actually *being there*. The vast hollow plane stretched dimly into shadow, no seats, no carpet, no paneling. As the pilot flew TOC, Sitz could *feel* the airplane's shuddering, "hear the big engines slowly revving up on one side and dying down on the other."[62]

"Hey, this is what test pilots do every day," John Burken remembers thinking when he peered out the MD-11's cockpit windows. As an engineer, he realized, "you get numbed—and probably you shouldn't." Burken has a sharp memory of summer turbulence over Arizona. "It was a very hot day, Yuma in August," he recalls. "The engineers were at the monitors in back and the monitors were rocking back and forth. One man was turning greener and greener."[63] During these experiments, one engineer attached to the project refused to go up on the flight tests, and once when he was scheduled, anxiety so overwhelmed him that he became physically ill and checked into a hospital. But at the personal level, he too reached his small triumph — eventually, he went along on a research flight.

After the successful landing in August, Dana Purifoy substituted for Fullerton as research pilot and in September flew the MD-11 to an airspace over the Pacific the pilots call "Whiskey Area," an emptiness where few commercial airliners fly and where pilots are able to do freeflight with few air-traffic-control constraints and with no compromise. Here after tests of PCA engagement at altitude and tests on center-of-gravity issues, the crew completely shut down two hydraulic systems. The airplane's control surfaces assumed an asymmetric position, and trim speed increased. But PCA still dominated with rough control. The final step in these

---

[62] Joel Sitz, interview with author, 18 June 1998.

[63] Burken interview.

investigations, however, did not come until two months later when Fullerton returned to flight over the desert beyond Edwards.[64]

In November, Fullerton took the MD-11 on a flight out over the Mojave to test PCA with absolutely no hydraulics. For Burcham, this trip was ultimate. He himself always downplays any humanitarian angle, insisting that the crash of Flight 232 at Sioux City is a mere locus in the chain of events, but the evidence is, Flight 232 is a benchmark. When the MD-11 tests were arranged, Burcham had the engine at the tail pulled back near idle and the two wing engines provided thrust control, the very configuration of Flight 232. As the technology developed, Burcham went out of his way to invite pilots Dennis Fitch and Al Haynes to try out PCA in simulations at Dryden and Ames. When any guest pilot went up, Burcham first handed the flier the situation that existed in midair out over Iowa in 1989.[65]

Behind Burcham's data sheets, the flow charts, diagrams, and equations, there was, if you stopped to look, a vision, a memory of the crippled transport in its bizarre journey; behind the benevolently

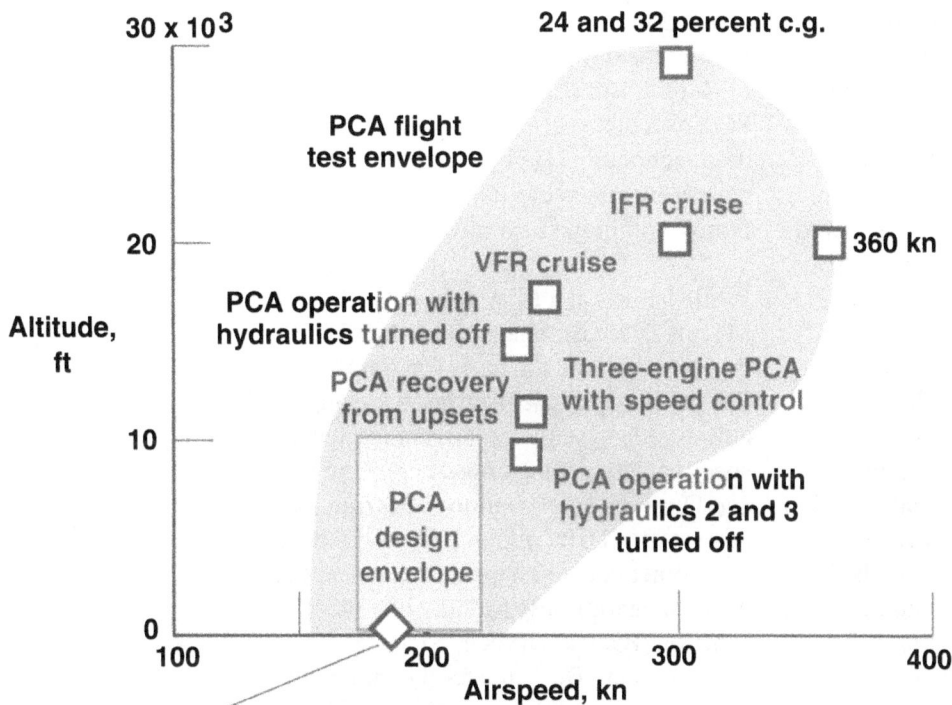

Figure 20. Diagram showing how much the flight envelope for the MD-11 expanded (in terms of altitude in feet and speed in knots) during flight research.

- PCA landings
- PCA approaches with no flaps, slots only, and rudder offset
- PCA ILS-coupled autolands
- Demonstration to 16 pilots; airlines, DoD, FAA, and industry

[64] The account of the Whiskey Area flight is based on interviews with Burcham, Miller, and Maine.

[65] Although I could list other test procedures that duplicate the circumstances of Flight 232, that might belabor the point. To be fair, there is another viewpoint about the motivation for using only two engines for thrust control. Trindel Maine wrote to this point in the original draft of this study: "Note: one of the major motivations for putting most of our PCA development effort on the MD-11 into just the two wing engine configuration with the center engine pulled back was to keep the research generic and applicable to other airplanes. Building a system that was critically dependent on the center engine would not easily be generalized to the much more common matched pairs of wing engines only [in the commercial transport fleet]. We didn't want to design a system solely for the MD-11; we wanted to demonstrate a general capability."

shaped curves of the phugoid in reports, a remembrance of something else, the twisting frantic rush of the airplane at impact, its bent metal gouging an 18-inch-deep hole along 4000 feet of Runway 22 at Sioux Gateway airport.

For the last hydraulics-off test on 28 November 1995, a third pilot, Ralph Luczak, joined the PCA team in the center seat of the cockpit. While Miller and Fullerton handled the controls, Luczak switched off the hydraulics systems—first each one separately, next each combination of two, and finally all three systems. And then the team sat, waiting to see what the result would be. The elevators did not move at all. The ailerons moved up, outboard aileron at 12 degrees and the inboard one less than half as much. The rudder did not budge. It was not a catastrophe, but these floating surfaces resulted in a nose-up pitch and caused a lower trim airspeed, the opposite of what had been predicted. The investigators had prepared to deal with the reverse. Because airspeed was then trimmed near minimum for flaps-up flight, they briefly turned a hydraulic pump on to increase speed. Once this was accomplished, Luczak again cut off all hydraulics, and after reaching a stable speed of 212 knots, the pilots proceeded with the test cards. They lowered the landing gear with an emergency system not requiring hydraulic pressure. The speed dropped another 17 knots. They flew a landing approach at altitude, and the track and pitch controls behaving normally.

The test was done.

Since these triumphs, PCA has taken a different path. If the technology gets attached to commercial airplanes, PCA must survive FAA certification. On the last day of the MD-11 demonstrations, an FAA guest pilot addressed this step. "Conceptually . . . a very good idea. This demonstration effectively shows the potential for practical implementation," wrote the FAA's Tom Imrich, adding, "more work is needed in order to move to the regulatory credit stage."[66]

One regulatory stage obstacle was retrofitting. PCA technology requires aircraft with full authority digital engine controls, a modification that is the wave of the future. Unfortunately, two thirds of the airplanes now in commercial airline fleets do not yet have these advanced controls, and these airplanes will remain operational for perhaps twenty-five years. For legal reasons, the industry will not mandate safety regulations on only a fraction of the fleet. Many observers noted this problem even as they applauded the MD-11 demonstrations—they viewed the day as a glimpse into the far-off future. But Burcham refused to look at PCA as a this-will-benefit-your-grandchildren technology. He believed it could benefit members of your immediate family within the next few years.

While he was at a PCA design review in May of 1995, Burcham hit on the idea that later became the basis for simpler PCA systems. Most airplanes have an autothrottle system to maintain a selected speed, much like the cruise control in a car. During a conversation about training costs with a Delta pilot, he first sketched, on another cocktail napkin, the concept of using an autothrottle for the pitch PCA function. Back at Dryden, controls engineer John Burken later did an analysis suggesting that the autothrottle could do almost as well as the full PCA system in controlling pitch.

Burcham later used this modified system to eliminate the need for changes to the engine control software. Most newer airplanes have not only an autothrottle system but also a digital thrust trim system. At first Burcham called the new approach "simplified PCA," but Ken Szalai soon re-christened it "PCA Lite."

---

[66] Tom Imrich, unpublished NASA Dryden pilot test cards, 30 November 1995.

To operate in PCA Lite, Burcham decided to run the pitch control through the autothrottle and use the engine thrust trim system, which despite a plus or minus five percent limit,[67] had enough range laterally for landing.

After the MD-11 tests concluded, PCA entered a new stage of development with the Dryden researchers working in close partnership with researchers at the NASA Ames Research Center in the Silicon Valley. Ames provided advanced simulation testbeds with dramatically realistic effects. Led by John Bull, a NASA veteran now working for CAELUM Research Corporation, these researchers developed an effective full PCA system for the Boeing 747. They also ran tests with great success demonstrating PCA on simulations for generic commercial airliner models. When Burcham requested sim tests for PCA Lite, Bull and his colleagues produced effective demonstrations. Tests confirmed they could expand the number of airplanes available for PCA, make this new version cheaper, and fly reasonably well with PCA Lite.[68]

The older airplanes that did not have digital engine controls required a different solution. The next innovation addressed airplanes having autothrottle but no engine thrust trim system. Burcham called it "PCA Ultralite," an arrangement requiring the pilot to manually operate the throttles for lateral control—a possible but difficult workload. PCA Ultralite by itself did not work well, but the Dryden-Ames team added an improvement, using the flight director needle in the cockpit. This step allowed the pilot to get effective lateral control by moving the throttles based on cues on the flight director

needle. Pilot evaluations at Ames in 1998 confirmed the results.

After successful Lite and Ultralite demonstrations, much remained to sift. The requirements of FAA certification are as complex and multilevel as the product it safeguards. Certification was not one big test. Rather, it was a proliferation of smaller tests, crucial in every case. Since the MD-11 days, the researchers have experimented on the C-17, a military jet transport that in many ways is characteristic of the next generation of large airplane. They have flown extensive Boeing 747 and Boeing 757 simulations. Experiments have included flying TOC tests on the U.S. Navy F-18. This new stage of experiment has involved flying many airplanes, dealt with a great variety of damages and looked at employing PCA as one element in post-catastrophe reconfiguration. The engineers have shown how a commercial airliner without flight controls and without an operating engine on one wing can engage PCA by using fuel transfer to offset the center of gravity toward the operating engine. John Bull and his colleagues at NASA Ames have fashioned a brilliant sim demonstration: the Boeing 747 has its hydraulics fail at 35,000 feet, rolls until it is upside down, and then the PCA mode is engaged. The airplane rights itself, levels its wings, and comes in for a safe landing nearly identical to a normal auto landing.[69]

If PCA prevails, however, it will not be because of brilliant technology. As many observers will tell you, the decision will be political, and in a multibillion-dollar industry and regulatory web, "political" means financial.

---

[67] That is, plus or minus five percent of the full range of engine operation.

[68] See Frank W. Burcham, *Using Engine Thrust for Emergency Flight Control: MD-11 and B-747 Results* (Edwards, CA: NASA TM -1998-206552, May 1998).

[69] The sources for this section are mostly interviews with Maine and Burcham. Also see John Bull, *Piloted Simulation Tests of Propulsion Control as a Backup to Loss of Primary Flight Controls for a Mid-Size Jet Transport* (Moffett Field, CA: NASA TM 110374, 1995).

PCA is inexpensive technology. Burcham and his colleagues have transformed a catastrophic scenario without adding any hardware to most transport airplanes. The expenses are software modification and training. But how much are aviation companies willing to spend on a backup system for a remote possibility of catastrophe? After the Flight 232 crash landing, the airplane manufacturer corrected

difficulties landing in heavy turbulence. But do you judge a safety backup by the standards of a normal landing? Would you judge a parachute's descent by the industry-standard for an airframe's landing? At the end of the MD-11 project, Jeff Kahler performed some risk calculations based on the sum of the guest pilot approaches, go-rounds, and simulation studies. He calculated that 96 landings would have

Figure 21. Gordon Fullerton in the Boeing 747 simulator at NASA's Ames Research Center. (NASA photo AC97-0295-15 by Tom Trower).

the system, but it is a partial-control fix and reports persist that pilots who train to use it encounter difficulties. The industry attitude concerning the Sioux City crash has been: "This will never happen again." The real question is, how remote is remote?

Ultimately, how will the FAA review this new technology? If PCA is judged against the yardstick of normal control-surface landings, it has shortcomings. The engineers have not yet resolved, for instance, some limits on its lateral response and

been rated safe landings and four would not, although these were "survivable." Kahler figured that in 100 attempts, PCA provided 100 survivable landings.[70]

If you should ever find yourself a passenger on a commercial airliner that has lost all hydraulics or flight controls, how satisfied could you be with your 50/50 chance of a crash landing when a technology was available which offered 100 out of 100 survivable landings? Although no one wants to anticipate a major catastrophe, the commercial aviation world may

---

[70] Jeff Kahler, interview by telephone with author, 24 June 1998.

Figure 22. Bill Burcham's Ultralite napkin showing the basic concept for PCA Ultralite; CLAWS stands for control laws; A/T means autothrottle; the symbols along the horizontal line at the bottom of the diagram stand for flightpath angle, flightpath angle rate, and airspeed. (NASA photo EC98-44690-1 by Brent Wood).

have its eyes on this one. A major disaster may cost nowadays, it has been estimated, nearly a billion dollars. But if there should ever occur another hydraulics-loss crash—there have been more than a half dozen in the last generation—given the stacks of reports on PCA, the wide industry awareness, the damage-suit lawyers would stand up before juries and have a field day.

In the end, economy may decide. But it may or may not be lawsuit economy. Dana Purifoy looks ahead to a PCA system that is "not a stand alone, but an integrated flight control."[71] Some observers see PCA as a backup to replace one of the backup hydraulic systems. Because PCA is only software, the savings in

airplane weight would result in significant fuel savings. One study shows cost savings of 140 million dollars for a fleet of 300 airplanes.

Many of the decisions about PCA will be made by players in an industry that rarely shows its hand or explains decision factors. But the NASA team is optimistic this safety backup technology will prevail. Burcham, continuing to refine PCA, merely shrugs, "I just hope it never has to be used." Other researchers look back on their roles in PCA's development and at the same time view it from a human angle and voice a great deal of pride. "I know someday I will see this implemented," says Joe Conley, "and it's going to save the lives of many people."[72]

---

[71] Purifoy interview.

[72] Conley interview.

Appendices

Appendix A

Aircraft Accident Report
United Airlines Flight 232
Sioux Gateway Airport
Sioux City, Iowa
July 19, 1989

"About 1 hour and 7 minutes after takeoff [in a DC-10]. . . the flightcrew heard a loud bang or an explosion, followed by vibration and a shuddering of the airframe. After checking the engine instruments, the flightcrew determined that the No. 2 aft (tail-mounted) engine had failed." The crew soon determined further that there was no hydraulic pressure to operate the normal flight controls.

After the flight attendants had informed the passengers of the problem and plans to attempt a landing at Sioux Gateway Airport, "a flight attendant advised the captain that a UAL [United Airlines] DC-10 training check airman [pilot who checks the proficiency of other airline pilots], who was off duty and seated in a first class passenger seat, had volunteered his assistance. The captain immediately invited the airman to the cockpit. . . ."

The check pilot ascertained that the flight control surfaces were not moving, so the captain directed him "to take control of the throttles to free" him and the first officer "to manipulate the flight controls."

The check airman attempted to use engine power to control pitch and roll. He said that the airplane had a continuous tendency to turn right, making it difficult to maintain a stable pitch attitude. He also advised that the No. 1 and No. 3 engine[1] thrust levers could not be used symmetrically, so he used two hands to manipulate the two throttles."

At this time (about 26 minutes after the explosion), the second officer inspected the tail area and reported "damage to the right and left horizontal stabilizers."

Fuel was jettisoned to the level of the automatic system cutoff, leaving 33,500 pounds. About 11 minutes before landing, the landing gear was extended by means of the alternate gear extension procedure."

The flight crew reported that it sighted the airport "about 9 miles out. ATC [air traffic control] had intended for flight 232 to attempt to land on runway 31, which was 8,999 feet long. However, ATC advised that the airplane was on approach to runway 22, which was closed. . . ." It said "that the length of this runway was 6,600 feet. Given the airplane's position and the difficulty in making left turns, the captain elected to continue the approach to runway 22 rather than to attempt maneuvering to runway 31." The check pilot stated his belief that "the airplane was lined up and on a normal glidepath to the field. The flaps and slats remained retracted."

"During the final approach, the captain recalled getting a high sink rate alarm from the ground proximity warning system (GPWS). In the last 20 seconds before touchdown, the airspeed averaged 215" knots as indicated by the aircraft's instruments, "and the sink rate was 1,620 feet per minute. Smooth oscillations in pitch and roll continued until just before touchdown when the right wing dropped rapidly." At "about 100 feet above the ground [according to the captain's statement] the nose of the airplane began to pitch downward. He also felt the right wing drop down about the same time. Both the captain and the first officer called for reduced power on short final approach."

---

[1] These engines were on the left and right wings, respectively.

The check pilot "said that based on experience with no flap/no slat approaches[,] he knew that power would have to be used to control the airplane's descent. He used the first officer's airspeed indicator and visual cues to determine the flightpath and the need for power changes. He thought that the airplane was fairly well aligned with the runway during the latter stages of the approach and that they would reach the runway." However, "soon thereafter, he observed that the airplane was positioned to the left of the desired landing area and descending at a high rate. He also observed that the right wing began to drop." He manipulated "the No. 1 and No. 3 engine throttles until the airplane contacted the ground. He said that no steady application of power was used on the approach and that the power was constantly changing. He believed that he added power just before contacting the ground."

"The airplane touched down on the threshold slightly to the left of the centerline on runway 22 at" some 44 minutes after the explosion. "The first ground contact was made by the right wing tip[,] followed by the right main landing gear. The airplane skidded to the right of the runway and rolled to an inverted position." Witnesses said the airplane ignited and did a cartwheel, "coming to rest after crossing runway 17/35. Firefighting and rescue operations began immediately, but the airplane was destroyed by impact and fire."

"Injuries to Persons

Injuries	Crew	Passengers	Other	Total
Fatal	1	110	0	111
Serious	6	41*	0	47
Minor	4	121	0	125
None	0	13	0	13
Total	11	285	0	296

* One passenger died 31 days after the accident as a result of injuries he had received in the accident. In accordance with legal precedent, "his injuries were classified 'serious.'"

Source: Quoted and paraphrased from National Transportation Safety Board Aircraft Accident Report, *United Airlines Flight 232* (Washington, DC: PB90-910406 NTSB/AAR-90/06, 1 Nov. 1990), pp. 1-5.

Appendix B

Flight Simulator Studies

As a result of the accident, the Safety Board directed a simulator reenactment of the events leading to the crash. The purpose of this effort was to replicate the accident airplane dynamics to determine if DC-10 flightcrews could be taught to control the airplane and land safely with no hydraulic power available to actuate the flight controls. The simulator exercise was based only on the situation that existed in the Sioux City accident—the failure of the No. 2 (center) engine and the loss of fluid for all three hydraulic systems.

The DC-10 simulator used in the study was programmed with the aerodynamic characteristics of the accident airplane that were validated by comparison with the actual flight recorder data. The DC-10 rated pilots, consisting of line captains, training clerk airmen, and production test pilots[,] were then asked to fly the accident airplane profile. Their comments, observations, and performance were recorded and analyzed. The only means of control for the flight crew was from the operating wing engines. The application of asymmetric power to the wing engines changed the roll attitude, hence the heading. Increasing and decreasing power had a limited effect on the pitch attitude. The airplane tended to oscillate about the center of gravity (CG) in the pitch axis. It was not possible to control the pitch oscillations with any measure of precision. Moreover, because airspeed is primarily determined by pitch trim configuration, there was no direct control of airspeed. Consequently, landing at a predetermined point and airspeed on a runway was a highly random event.

Overall, the results of this study showed that such a maneuver involved many unknown variables and was not trainable, and the degree of controllability during the approach and landing rendered a simulator training exercise virtually impossible. However, the results of these simulator studies did provide some advice that may be helpful to flight crews in the extremely unlikely event that they are faced with a similar situation. This information has been presented to the industry by the Douglas Aircraft Company in the form of an "All DC-10 Operators Letter." In addition to discussing flight control with total hydraulic failure, the letter describes a hydraulic system enhancement mandated by an FAA Airworthiness Directive. . . .

Source: Quoted from National Transportation Safety Board Aircraft Accident Report, *United Airlines Flight 232* (Washington, DC: PB90-910406 NTSB/AAR-90/06, 1 Nov. 1990), pp. 72-73.

Appendix C

National Transportation Safety Board Recommendation

Encourage research and development of backup flight control systems for newly certified wide-body airplanes that utilize an alternative source of motive power separate from that source used for the conventional control system. (Class II, Priority Action) (A-10-168)

Source: Quoted from National Transportation Safety Board Aircraft Accident Report, *United Airlines Flight 232* (Washington, DC: PB90-910406 NTSB/AAR-90/06, 1 Nov. 1990), p. 102.

Appendix D

Guest Pilot Comments on
the Propulsion Controlled Aircraft System
Flown on the F-15 Highly Integrated
Digital Electronic Control Aircraft

A group of propulsion-controlled aircraft [PCA] guest pilots, who flew the F-15 equipped with PCA, were all test pilots; their comments and recommendations for added features are presented here. . . . [Note: Some of the guest pilots worked at NASA Dryden, and their comments were so brief and non-specific that they were not included in the technical report from which these comments are taken. The comments included here go into greater detail and are representative of the tenor of the remaining comments.]

EXCERPTS FROM GUEST PILOT C

The evaluation was flown in clear weather with more than 30 n. mi. [nautical miles] visibility. Winds were at magnetic heading of 240° at a speed of 18 knots gusting to 26 knots. All approaches were flown to runway 22.

Control Augmentation System-Off Control

With the CAS [control augmentation system] off, the aircraft responded sluggishly in all axes. In addition, fine-tracking tasks were difficult to complete, and the completed task [was]only marginally adequate.

Throttles-Only Manual Control

Throttles-only manual flight was extremely difficult, if not impossible, without a large amount of training. The major problem was controlling the phugoid in pitch. The anticipation required to achieve such control was monumental. Using differential thrust to control roll was marginal at best, and it was fairly easy to use the wrong throttle when trying to control bank. The throttles-only manual flight condition was unsatisfactory and would not be recommended for use in any ejection-seat-equipped aircraft.

Propulsion-Controlled Aircraft System Control

The airplane responded adequately to all inputs commanded by the pilot. Pitch and roll response were very sluggish, yet always consistent and, therefore, predictable. The phugoid was suppressed by the system and was not noticeable except when making large changes in pitch. The dutch roll was well-controlled by the system. Generally, the system provided excellent flightpath stability and good control of the aircraft without being overly sensitive to gusts.

Unusual Attitude Recovery

The airplane was flown with the CAS off, at 250 *KCAS* [calibrated airspeed expressed in knots] and at an altitude of 10,000 ft m.s.l. [above mean sea level], to a −10° flightpath angle and then banked to approximately 75°. When this attitude was achieved, the flight controls were released, the inlets were selected to the emergency position, and the PCA system was engaged. Only the PCA system was used to recover the aircraft. Initially, a level flight attitude was selected at the thumbwheels. The aircraft pitched up and basically entered the phugoid mode, slowing down in the climb. Right bank was selected with the thumbwheels to aid the nosedrop and minimize the airspeed bleed off. While on the downswing of the phugoid motion, the gear and flaps were extended. This action was accomplished on the descending portion of the phugoid to minimize the effects of the increased pitching moment caused by flap extension. Unusual attitude recovery was easy and effective using the PCA system controls, and at no time was the pilot concerned about the aircraft position because of PCA system performance.

Instrument Descent

Two instrument descents were flown during the flight evaluation. The pitch response was solid. At this point, flightpath and speed stability were also good. The aircraft performance during these maneuvers was similar to those observed in basic autopilots capable of speed and attitude hold.

Final Approach

Four approaches were attempted with the full PCA system. A visual approach to a safe position from which to land was consistently achieved using the PCA system.

Go-Around

A go-around using the PCA system was completed during the PCA system approach to 100 ft *AGL* [above ground level]. The PCA system allowed a timely and safe go-around without requiring undue pilot effort or skill.

EXCERPTS FROM GUEST PILOT D

The weather at engine start included a scattered-cloud layer at 6000 ft, winds at a heading of 230[°] and a speed of 14 knots, and light turbulence from the surface to an altitude of 8000 ft. Turning all three CAS axes off and selecting the emergency position for the pitch and the roll ratios resulted in the expected: very sloppy handling characteristics. The airplane was difficult to trim in the roll and pitch axes. The pitch axis required a larger than expected amount of noseup trim to stabilize at 150 *KCAS*. Once trimmed, the pilot released the control stick and attempted to maintain level flight and capture a heading by manually adjusting the throttles. Even though the air was very smooth at these 8000- to 9000-ft m.s.l. test conditions, aircraft control was very poor. The velocity vector varied ± 4°, and the pilot overshot the intended heading by 7°. Rather than continuing to try to fine-tune this manual control, the pilot engaged the PCA system. The immediate increase in airplane controllability was very dramatic. Small flightpath angle changes to a maximum of 2° were made very accurately, and the first heading capture attempt was only overshot by 2°. The second PCA approach was to 100 ft *AGL* at 150 *KCAS* and an 11° angle of attack and included a PCA system-controlled go-around. During the approach, the pilot could hear the engines winding up and down, but the ride quality was quite smooth. On this approach, the pilot initially biased the airplane upwind of the runway to compensate for the crosswind. The pilot overcompensated and had to perform a sidestep to the left. That sidestep maneuver was easy to perform. The engine speed was matched for this approach, and the roll command no longer had to be biased one way or another.

Even though the overall turbulence seemed very similar to the previous approach, two or three upsets occurred that seemed larger than the previous approach and actually displaced the flightpath laterally. These upsets emphasized the observation that the pilot workload was significantly higher in the roll axis than in the pitch axis. From a –2° flightpath, pilot D used the PCA system to command a 10° flightpath angle go-around at 100 ft *AGL*. The minimum altitude during this go-around was 60 ft *AGL*. The airplane quickly started climbing, and the pilot had to aggressively command level flight to keep from climbing into conflicting traffic overhead. At the end of the maneuver, the pilot was level at an altitude of 2800 ft (500 ft *AGL*). All in all, the approach was very comfortable. Pilot D had good control over the aim point and had reasonably good control over the heading of the flightpath. The third PCA system approach was flown to 50 ft *AGL* at 140 *KCAS*, then uncoupled with the PCA engage/uncouple button and then hand-flown through a CAS-off PARRE [pitch and roll ratios emergency] (the button is located on the right throttle) touch-and-go landing. The winds were at a heading of 230° at a speed of 19 knots gusting to 24 knots. The pilot's overwhelming conclusion from this approach was that the PCA system easily has sufficient authority and controllability for straight-in approaches and for navigational maneuvers (provided the gear and flaps are down). The presence of the velocity vector on the HUD [head-up display] was also a tremendous aid. During the approach, the pilot got low and dragged in. As if that wasn't enough, the pilot also got a large upset from turbulence at approximately 250 ft *AGL*. At that time, the pilot made a large correction to get back on the desired flightpath. That correction bottomed out at 160 ft *AGL* and then peaked at 230 ft *AGL*. At that point, the pilot reestablished a 2.5° glideslope and continued with the approach. Despite this large and very late correction, the only penalty suffered was the intended touchdown point shifted from 500 ft down the runway to 2000 ft down the runway. Of all the maneuvers performed during the flight, that last-minute correction impressed the pilot more than anything else. Pilot D was very pleased with the robustness and the ability of the PCA system to handle that large of a correction in such a short time. The final approach was to 200 ft *AGL* at 140 *KCAS* using throttles-only manual control. The workload during the manual approach was extremely high. The pilot had worked up a sweat on the last [manual] approach. Approaching the runway, pilot D got behind on the pitch corrections, and the flightpath angle ballooned to 6°. The subsequent pitchdown correction dropped to −7°. The pilot still did not have this large pitch change under control using the throttles alone, so as the flightpath angle started passing up through level flight, the pilot took over manually at 200 ft *AGL*. This manual approach was not landable.

Summary

From the ground training and the demonstration profile to the PCA control law implementation, this PCA system demonstration was very well-done. More than simply a proof-of-concept demonstrator, this flight exhibited capabilities that would enhance the survivability of aircraft. As long as aircraft have failure modes where the ability to fly the airplane with the control stick or yoke may be lost, this pilot would like to have the backup capability demonstrated by the PCA system.

EXCERPTS FROM GUEST PILOT E

This flight was an evaluation flight of the F-15 PCA system. The weather was good, winds were light, and little or no turbulence existed. After takeoff and a climb to an altitude of 7500 ft m.s.l., a short pilot evaluation was flown with the airplane in the landing configuration, with inlets in the emergency position, and with the CAS off. Pitch and roll ratios were also in the emergency position. Trim speed was 150 *KCAS*. This evaluation "warmed up" the pilot for throttles-only flying by allowing exposure to a degraded landing configuration. In addition, the evaluation was useful in demonstrating the somewhat sluggish and imprecise basic handling of the unaugmented F-15 airplane.

Throttles-Only Manual Control

Before approaches with the PCA system engaged, an up-and-away evaluation was flown with manual throttle control. Up-and-away manual control of heading and changes in vertical flightpath were achieved with a high degree of pilot workload. Many rapid, large, symmetric and asymmetric throttle movements were necessary, few of which seemed intuitive. A satisfactory, yet imprecise, job of up-and-away control was accomplished providing that corrections were made in a single axis. A large effort was required to damp the phugoid motion. In addition, small precise throttle movements were hindered by the very large amounts of throttle friction. A throttles-only manual approach was flown but aborted at less than 1000 ft *AGL* when pitch control was lost during an attempt to make a lineup correction to the runway.

Coupled Approaches

Engaging the PCA system and flying with it for several minutes provides a remarkable contrast to using throttles-only manual control. Steep bank angles (25°) can be flown with full confidence, and precise (±1°) heading and flightpath angle changes can be performed. Pilot[s'] confidence in their ability to conduct an approach increases greatly. The tendency toward a very flat glideslope well before the threshold was finally corrected on the third approach. The correction required aggressively, yet smoothly, driving the velocity vector in pitch by overdriving the command box. Then, some of the commanded input was taken out when the velocity vector neared the desired position. Laterally, a series of nearly constant small corrections was required to maintain heading.

Coupled Waveoff

On the second approach to 100 ft *AGL*, a go-around was initiated using only the PCA pitch thumbwheel. By rolling the command box to an approximately 7° noseup pitch attitude, the control system added power and flew the aircraft away with the roundout before the climb occurred at approximately 70 ft. This maneuver was straight-forward and demonstrated another impressive system capability.

Summary

Overall, the PCA system on the F-15 airplane is a breakthrough technology that is strongly recommended for incorporation in future or current aircraft. The system gives the pilot the ability to control and safely land an aircraft that otherwise would crash or be abandoned before landing.

EXCERPTS FROM GUEST PILOT G

The flight was flown in the morning, but a significant crosswind and light turbulence existed. After takeoff, pilot G flew the basic airplane CAS[control augmentation system]-off card. As expected, the airplane had poor stability, had very light damping, rolled off quickly, was hard to trim, and was sluggish because of high stick forces. When the PCA system was turned on, the pilot's comment was "PCA flies the airplane really well. The thumbwheel concept is good, and the gains are just right." On the first approach, pilot G commented that "the airplane was real stable. I was surprised at how well the PCA held glideslope. The roll response was really good." On the PCA system go-around, the airplane was at a –3° glideslope at 100 ft *AGL* [above ground level], but the pilot put in a big noseup command. The comment was "I was confident of the go-around, which bottomed out 60 ft above the ground." On the next approach to 50 ft *AGL*, the pilot had a very nice approach going and said, "I think you could get the airplane on the ground from this approach in spite of the crosswind." The pilot then did the simulated hydraulic failure upset at an altitude of 10,000 ft, with a 90° bank and 20° dive, and engaged the PCA system. The system rolled out aggressively, pulled approximately 3 *g* [equivalent of the force of gravity] in the pull-out, and recovered nicely to level flight. The pilot accidentally bumped the stick, which disengaged the system. This action prevented a full PCA system descent and approach, but the pilot had no doubts that the test could have been completed. Then pilot G tried a throttles-only manual approach, and, like all the guest pilots, had no success at all. The pilot did manage to get the runway in sight but had to use the stick occasionally to maintain control.

EXCERPTS FROM GUEST PILOT H

The PCA system flown in the HIDEC F-15 airplane was evaluated as a highly effective backup recovery system for aircraft that totally lose conventional flight controls. The system was simple and intuitive to use and would require only minimal training for pilots to learn to use effectively. Of course, landing using the PCA system would require higher workloads than normal, but this pilot believes landings could be done safely. The fact that the system provides a simple, straight-forward, go-around capability that allows multiple approaches further supports its safe landing capability. The dutch-roll suppression characteristics of the system were extremely impressive to the pilot and would allow landings to be done even in nonideal wind conditions. The pilot thought the PCA system exhibited great promise and, if incorporated into future transport aircraft, could further improve the safety of the passenger airlines.

Control Augmentation System-Off Control

Shortly after takeoff, the aircraft was placed in the powered-approach configuration while flying straight and level at an altitude of 6200 ft mean sea level (m.s.l.). Pilot workload in the CAS-off mode was high, and control precision was marginal. The F-15 airplane felt sluggish in pitch and roll and was difficult to trim. The airplane felt like a "heavier" aircraft because of slow response to [pilot's] inputs and heavy stick forces. The pilot had to shape or lead inputs to capture desired bank or pitch angles. Rudder doublets excited a moderately damped dutch roll.

Manual Throttles-Only Control

Overall controllability was adequate with throttle manipulation. Bank-angle control was intuitive and fairly easy to accomplish. Collective throttle movement provided marginally adequate pitch-angle control in the F-15 airplane. Controlling one axis at a time was not too difficult, but maintaining simultaneous control of pitch and roll required all of the pilot's attention. Overall, throttles-only manual control would probably allow the pilot to return to friendly territory, but pilot fatigue and task saturation could occur. The PCA system control and approach tests are described next.

Control

The PCA system provided satisfactory control of pitch and roll axes. Bank-angle capture was generally good with an approximately 2° oscillation about the desired bank angle. This oscillation was likely caused by turbulence or gust response because dutch roll appeared to be well-damped by the PCA system. Flightpath angle captures were successful using the pitch thumbwheel to position the HUD flightpath command box. Overall, the pilot was impressed with the capability of the PCA system and the reduction in pilot workload it afforded. A pilot could easily accomplish several other tasks while flying the aircraft in this mode.

Approach to 200 ft Above Ground Level

Pitch control was outstanding, which allowed the pilot to work almost exclusively in the roll axis. Pilot workload in roll was high; however, the workload could have been significantly reduced if a "heading hold" feature was incorporated. Overall pilot confidence in the PCA system during this first approach was high.

Recovery from Unusual Attitude and Descent to Approach to 20 ft Above Ground Level

This point was entered at 260 knots calibrated airspeed (*KCAS*) and an altitude of 10,200 ft m.s.l. [feet above mean sea level]. The gear and flaps were up, and the inlets were in the automatic scheduling mode. The CAS was off, and pitch and roll ratios were in the emergency position. The aircraft was then maneuvered to 90° left wing down and 10° nosedown. Next, the pilot positioned the inlets to the emergency position to simulate hydraulic failure and engaged the PCA system. The nose continued to drop until the wings leveled approximately 5 sec later. Maximum airspeed during the pullout was 360 *KCAS*. After two phugoid cycles, the oscillatory motion was damped by the PCA system. In addition, the aircraft stabilized at 150 *KCAS*. A straight-in approach was flown to runway 22 in winds at a magnetic heading of 280° and a speed of 10 knots in light turbulence. Aggressive roll thumb-wheel action resulted in good lineup control. One item of concern was a slight pitchdown that occurred as the airplane passed 30 ft *AGL*. This pitchdown appeared to be similar to the ground effect-induced pitchdown encountered on the initial PCA system landings conducted by NASA pilots. Overall, the ability of the PCA system to recover the aircraft from an unusual attitude at 260 *KCAS* and then provide satisfactory approach control at a trim airspeed of 150 *KCAS* was impressive.

Manual Throttles-Only Approach to 200 ft Above Ground Level

This straight-in approach was flown to runway 22 in winds at a magnetic heading of 280° and a speed of 8 knots in light turbulence. The F-15 manual mode (throttles only, no augmentation) was unacceptable for flying a safe or repeatable approach to landing.

Conclusions

Overall, the PCA concept demonstrates good potential for use as a backup flight control system for tactical naval aircraft. The system provides adequate control authority for the F-15A airplane and enables repeatable, safe approaches without the use of conventional mechanical flight controls. The pilot was impressed with the ability of the system to precisely control bank and flightpath angles. Pilot workload throughout the PCA-coupled approaches was low relative to the throttles-only manual approach. This low workload was convincing testimony to the value of the PCA system. An aircraft employing the PCA system as the sole backup flight control system would be able to save considerable weight by eliminating typical hydromechanical backups.

Source: Quoted with minor editing in brackets from Frank W. Burcham, Jr., Trindel A. Maine, C. Gordon Fullerton, and Lannie Dean Webb, *Development and Flight Evaluation of an Emergency Digital Flight Control System Using Only Engine Thrust on an F-15 Airplane* (Edwards, CA: NASA Technical Paper 3627, 1996), pp. 93-97.

Appendix E

PCA System Landing
in an MD-11 Aircraft
29 August 1995

The MD-11 was flown to Edwards AFB, where a 15,000-ft long, 300-ft wide runway was used for initial PCA landing attempts. Pilot A flew three PCA low approaches to gradually lower altitude PCA system go-arounds. Continuous light turbulence and occasional upsets from thermals occurred; however, PCA performance was judged adequate to proceed to PCA landings. On the first intended landing, initial lineup and flightpath control were good. Based on simulation experience, the pilot selected a flightpath of –1° at 140 ft AGL [above ground level]. The flightpath overshot to approximately –0.5° and then began to decrease back through the –1° command. At 30 ft AGL, the sink rate was increasing to 8 ft/sec, so the safety pilot, as briefed, made a small nose-up elevator input, then allowed the airplane to touch down under PCA system control. The touchdown was 25 ft left of the runway centerline, 5000 ft from the threshold at a sink rate of 4.5 ft/sec. The MD-11 was stopped using reverse thrust and brakes but no spoilers or nosewheel steering.

The second landing was accomplished using a slightly different flightpath control technique. Pilot A made small track changes to maintain runway lineup and set the flightpath command at –1.9° for the initial part of the approach. Airspeed was 175 kn[ots] at 200 ft AGL, based on the experience with the first landing, the pilot shallowed the flightpath to –1°, and at 100 ft to –0.5°. The airplane touched down smoothly on the centerline at a 4 ft/sec sink rate, 3000 ft from the threshold with no inputs from the safety pilot. Note [that there was an] upset from a thermal updraft that caused the airplane bank angle to increase to 8° at 100 ft AGL; the PCA track mode corrected without any pilot input. The airplane was stopped using reverse thrust and light braking but no flight control inputs. Pilot A rated the pitch control as excellent and the lateral control as adequate on this landing.

From the two landings in light turbulence, it was observed that PCA generally controlled track and pitch to within ±0.5° of command (disregarding the 1° bias in the track command). EPR [engine pressure ratio] values on approach were approximately 1.15, and variations were normally approximately ±0.1; a 0.4 EPR differential thrust was used to correct for the thermal upset. Ground effect was similar to that seen in the simulator.

Later in the day, additional Flaps 28 [with flaps at an angle of roughly 28°] approaches were conducted at Edwards AFB by pilot C. By this time, the afternoon turbulence activity had increased so much that the new pilot using the PCA mode had difficulty adequately maintaining a stable approach. Next, three approaches with flaps and slats retracted were conducted with a go-around at 200 ft AGL. The first approach was at Edwards, and the last two were at Yuma. The results from all three approaches indicated that the aircraft, using PCA system control, arrived at a suitable position to land on the runway. PCA system operation was also evaluated en route from Edwards to Yuma using all the PCA modes. Testing during this period included phugoid investigation, step responses, rudder trim offsets, and frequency sweeps.

The only significant problem encountered in PCA testing to this point was the sluggish and difficult-to-predict lateral control on approaches in turbulence. Pilots found that three or four approaches were required before adequate lineup was consistently achieved.

Source: Quoted with minor editing in brackets from Frank W. Burcham, Jr., John J. Burken, Trindel A. Maine, and C. Gordon Fullerton, *Development and Flight Test of an Emergency Flight Control System Using Only Engine Thrust on an MD-11 Transport Airplane* (Edwards, CA: NASA TP-97-206217, 1997), pp. 42-43.

Appendix F

Summary of
Guest Pilot Comments about
Flying PCA Approaches in an
MD-11 Aircraft
29-30 November 1995

PCA pilots and observers in MD-11

Name	Affiliation	Position
Pilots		
William Wainwright	Airbus Industrie	Chief test pilot
Kenneth Higgins	Boeing	Vice pres., flight operations
Tom McBroom, captain	American Airlines	Chief technical pilot
Roy Tucker, captain	Delta Airlines	MD-11 chief pilot
Chip Adam	Federal Aviation Admin.	Engineering pilot
Tom Imrich	Federal Aviation Admin.	NRS, air carrier ops
George Lyddane	Federal Aviation Admin.	NRS, flight mgt.
Carl Malone	Federal Aviation Admin.	Acrft. eval. group
Hiromichi Mitsuhashi, captain	Japan Air Lines	Asst. to dir. engrng.
Koci Sasaki, captain	Japan Air Lines	Deputy vice president
Abdullah Alhabdad, captain	Royal Flight (Saudi)	Vice pres., flt. ops.
Ruedi Bornhauser, captain	Swissair	Technical operations
Ed Allvin, captain	U.S. Air Force	AFFTC, 418th flight test force
Frank Batteas, Lt Col	U.S. Air Force	AFFTC
Bob Stoney, Lt Cdr	U.S. Navy	NATC TPS
Steve Wright, Cdr	U.S. Navy	NATC TPS
Gordon Fullerton	NASA Dryden	Project pilot
Dana Purifoy	NASA Dryden	PCA evaluation pilot
John Miller	McDonnell Douglas	MD-11 chief pilot
Ralph Luczak	McDonnell Douglas	PCA project pilot
Tom Melody	McDonnell Douglas	MDA chief pilot
Walt Smith	McDonnell Douglas	MD-11 PCA pilot
Tim Dineen	McDonnell Douglas	MD-11 pilot
Don Alexander	McDonnell Douglas	MD-11 pilot
Observers		
Robert Gilles	Airbus Industrie	Director, flight test
Mike Dornheim	Aviation Week	Technical writer
Ed Kolano	Flight International	Technical writer
John Bull	NASA Ames	PCA engineer
Don Bryant	NASA Ames	Simulation engineer
Larry Yount	Honeywell	Honeywell fellow
Tom Enyart	Federal Aviation Admin.	Pvt. pilot/engineer
Bill Dana	Chief engineer	NASA Dryden

Following the engagement of PCA, each pilot flew a downwind and base leg to a 12-mi straight-in approach [in the MD-11]. Each pilot then made a PCA approach to a virtual runway at 100 ft AGL [above ground level] (the first flare was set for 230 ft AGL and the second flare to 130 ft AGL). Most used the ILS-coupled mode, while a few used PCA FPA [flightpath angle] and TRK [track angle (magnetic heading of ground track)] control. In the very smooth air of these tests, even the PCA approaches using the FCP [flight control panel on cockpit glareshield] knobs were successful. At the 100-ft decision height, the pilots then pushed the TOGA [turnoff-go-around] button on the throttles to initiate a PCA go-around. The go-around was continued with a turn to the crosswind leg.

All pilots were very impressed with the PCA system. In general, FPA and TRK modes were preferred, although the bank angle mode and V/S [vertical speed] modes received very little evaluation. The pilots all were impressed with the go-around capability in which less than 60 ft of altitude were typically lost. These pilots also commented that control seemed almost normal and that, aside from the brief lateral acceleration immediately after making a track change, they could not tell whether the engines were providing all of the flight control. All pilots found the FCP knobs very easy and natural to use. Observers sitting in the cabin noted no difference from a normal approach unless seated where they could hear the engine sounds changing pitch.

The following excerpts from questionnaires summarize the demonstration pilot comments and suggestions for additional work:

1. Conceptually, a very good idea. This demonstration effectively shows the potential for practical implementation. More work is needed in order to move to the regulatory credit stage.

2. Basic PCA track/flightpath angle is excellent for all normal tasks. Use of fully coupled ILS/MLS [microwave landing system]/FMS [flight management system], etc., is the safest concept.

3. Pilotage with manual throttle consistently induced both phugoid and dutch roll tendencies. The insertion of PCA damped these modes out.

4. The PCA is an enhancing characteristic and will increase the level of safety of the aircraft. This technology should be further developed.

5. I had trouble flying manual with throttles only for pitch and roll. When on auto, it smoothed out. I think this program will be good for future backup systems, or partial control for normal systems.

6. Simulator evaluation was perfect setup to understand principles for PCA and see small throttle maneuvers. Aircraft was easier to fly in manual mode than simulator, but got better feel for phugoid in the aircraft. Controlled flight with autopilot more consistent than manual mode.

7. PCA manual track very controllable—smooth pitch corrections. Side force during turn initiation was noticeable but not objectionable. Pitch and glidepath angle were easily achieved using the thumbwheel. ILS was intercepted using this mode, and tracking, while requiring attention, was a nonevent.

8. Manual manipulation of throttles for pitch/roll control was very workload intensive. Bank control to within 5° moderately difficult. Pitch control extremely difficult. Utilization of track/bank and flightpath angle modes was impressive. These modes took a marginally controllable aircraft (especially in pitch) and made it extremely easy to fly.

9. Manual flying—to control phugoid, needed a couple of simulator approaches for experience. But when PCA engaged, it could be controlled perfectly. PCA flightpath angle control was smooth and better than expected.

10. Very useful demonstration of a system which shows good potential for use in some serious failure cases. An obvious limitation is that the system can only work (without the center engine) about a trim speed, which will vary with circumstances. Thus, its ability to maneuver is limited, but it works well on a well-constrained task such as a level entry to a glideslope with a small intercept angle to the localizer.

11. Aircraft very controllable in autopilot modes (PCA). Manually, control next to impossible. Coupled, very impressive—a safe landing should be possible.

12. Basically, takes what had been a very challenging, if not impossible, situation into what could be considered a textbook lesson with no exceptional pilot skills required.

13. Amazing! Overall, you have to see it to believe it! All involved people have done a great job.

14. I was amazed that the roll response was very quick and positive compared to the simulator. I experienced manual throttle control[;] PCA is very helpful.

15. Pitch and roll rates experienced with the PCA system engaged were comparable with those routinely used by the airlines. A small lateral acceleration was felt as the system commanded differential thrust. Noticeable, but not uncomfortable, this sideways pulse was only evident with roll initiation.

Source: Quoted with minor editing in brackets from Frank W. Burcham, Jr., John J. Burken, Trindel A. Maine, and C. Gordon Fullerton, *Development and Flight Test of an Emergency Flight Control System Using Only Engine Thrust on an MD-11 Transport Airplane* (Edwards, CA: NASA TP-97-206217, 1997), pp. 74-76.

Appendix G

Awards and Honors

The PCA team and project have received numerous awards and honors, including the following as of September 1997:

Discover Award for Technological Innovation, Finalist 1993

NASA Group Achievement Award, PCA project team, 19 Aug. 1993

Popular Science's "The Best of What's New," the year's 100 greatest Achievements In Science and Technology, 1993

Ray Temhoff award for best paper, Society of Experimental Test Pilots Symposium, Gordon Fullerton, 1993

Patent Award, US Patent #5,330,131 for Engines-Only Flight Control System. 19 July 1994

1994 R&D 100 awards for Propulsion Controlled Aircraft, 22 September 1994

NASA Exceptional Engineering Achievement Award 1994 (PCA)

NASA Tech Brief, 1995, Burcham, Fullerton, Gilyard, Conley, Stewart

1995 *Aviation Week & Space Technology* Laurel Award to Burcham and Fullerton, Jan. 1996

1995 NASA Commercial Invention of the Year Award & nominee for Government Invention of the Year Award

1997 AIAA Guidance, Navigation, and Control Conference Best Paper, MD-11 PCA Flight test results.

1997 Flight Safety Foundation Presidential Citation

1997 Patent Award for PCA-Lite

1997 (Best paper award), Burcham, Frank W., Sitz, Joel, and Bull, John: "Propulsion Controlled Aircraft: A Safety and Survivability Enhancement Concept," ADPA/NSIA Symposium Paper, 23 October 1997

Source: Information provided by Mr. Burcham.

Index

Acronyms, 5-7
Air Force, U.S., 14
Airplane crashes, 1-2
Ames Research Center, 29, 31, 32 ill.
Aviation Week & Space Technology, 1, 22

Barber, Marvin R. (Russ), 24-25
Baron, Robert S., 24
Boeing Aerospace Corporation, 14 n, 23
Boeing 720, 7
Boeing 747, 31
Boeing 757, 31
Bull, John S., 31, 50
Burcham, Frank W., 1, 2-32, 13 ill., 18 ill., 21
    ill., 27 ill., 50
Burken, John J., 6, 18, 24, 26, 28, 27 ill., 28, 30

C-5, 12
C-17, 31
Conley, Joseph L., 7, 11, 12, 27, 33, 50
Controlled Impact Demonstration (CID), 7
Control laws, 7-8
Control surfaces, 4, 15, 16, 19, 25, 26, 28, 30, 32
Crashes, 2, 12, 29-30, 32, 36-38

Deets, Dwain A., 23
Digital computers, 2, 14
Digital electronic engine controls, 14, 23, 30
Digital Electronic Flight Control System
    (DEFCS), 1 ill.
Douglas Aircraft, 24, 26, 28
Dryden Flight Research Center, 1, 3, 27 ill.,
    passim
Dutch roll, 4 ill.

Edwards Air Force Base, CA, 1, 3, 22, 26 ill., 27

F-4 Control Configured Vehicle (CCV), 15-16
F-15, 2 ill., 6 ill., 14, 15 ill., 16 ill., 17-18, 19 ill.,
    20 ill., 21 ill., 40-45
F-18, 31
Feather, John, 24, 27 ill.
Federal Aviation Administration (FAA), 5, 7, 30,
    31, 32
Fitch, Dennis, 2, 6, 11, 16, 29
Flight Control Computer (FCC), 14, 24
Flight research, 16-18, 20-22, 25-27, 28-30

Fullerton, Charles Gordon, 10-13, 13 ill., 15 ill.,
    15-18, 20 ill., 20-22, 21 ill., 26, 27 ill., 28-30,
    32 ill, 50
Funding, 10, 14, 24

General Electric, 24
Gilyard, Glenn B., 7-8, 21, 50
Ground effects, 19-20
Guest pilots, 22, 27-28, 40-45, 47-49

Hamilton, Len, 22
Haynes, Al, 2, 12-13, 13 ill., 16, 25, 29
Highly Integrated Digital Electronic Control
    (HIDEC), 1 ill., 2 ill., 3, 6, 14, 15
Honeywell, 24, 27
Hydraulic controls, 1, 19, 25

Imrich, Tom, 30
Inlet effects, 19
Instrument Landing System (ILS), 12, 27

Japan Airlines, 12

Kahler, Jeff, 24, 26, 27, 32
King, John, 23

Langley Research Center, 23
Lauber, John, 23
Le, Jeanette H., 7-8
Luczak, Ralph, 24, 29

Maine, Trindel A., 3 n, 18 ill., 19-20, 24
McDonnell Douglas Aerospace, 14, 19, 22, 23,
    24
MD-11, 22 ill., 23-30, 26 ill., 27 ill., 29 ill., 46-
    49
Miller, John, 24, 26, 28, 30

National Aeronautics and Space Administration,
    23; see also Ames, Dryden, Langley
National Transportation Safety Board (NTSB), 5,
    23, 38-39
Neighbor, Terry, 14

Pappas, Drew, 24-25, 27
Petersen, Kevin L., iv, 7
Phugoid oscillation, 3 ill., 4

Pratt & Whitney, 20, 24
Project managers, 24
Propulsion Controlled Aircraft (PCA) project,
    1 ill., 3 n, 4-33, 33 ill., 40-45
PCA Lite, 30-31
PCA Ultralite, 31, 33 ill.
Purifoy, Dana, 4, 10, 24, 28, 33

Risk calculations, 32

Simulation, 6 ill., 7-8, 10, 14-15, 18, 24, 18-20,
    24, 29, 30, 38
Sioux Gateway Airport, 2, 12, 30, 32, 36-38
Sitz, Joel R., 24, 28, 50
Skepticism about PCA, 9, 12, 18
Smith, Walt, 24
Stewart, James F., Dr., 2, 3-4, 5, 9, 11, 12, 13 ill.,
    50
Szalai, Kenneth J., 9-10, 30

Throttles Only Control (TOC), 7, 11, 16, 31
Thumbwheels, 11, 15-16, 26

Urnes, James, 14, 21, 22

Vietnam, 12

Wells, Edward, 14-15, 21
Whitehead, Robert E., Dr., 23
Wolf, Thomas D., 6, 15

Yeager, Bob, 16
Yuma, AZ, 26

About the Author

Tom Tucker is a writer who has a special interest in topics relating to invention. He is the author of *Brainstorm: The Stories of Twenty American Kid Inventors* (New York: Farrar, Straus & Giroux, 1995, revised 1998) and "Bolt of Fate: Benjamin Franklin and His Electric Kite Experiment" (due from Foreign Affairs Books in 2000). He has published in many periodicals and also has written about baseball, including a baseball short story featured in *Sports Illustrated*. He is an instructor at Isothermal Community College in Spindale, NC. He attended Harvard College and Washington University in St. Louis, earning his B.A. and later an M.A. on a Woodrow Wilson Fellowship at Washington University.

Monographs in Aerospace History

This is the sixteenth publication in a new series of special studies prepared under the auspices of the NASA History Program. The Monographs in Aerospace History series is designed to provide a wide variety of investigations relative to the history of aeronautics and space. These publications are intended to be tightly focused in terms of subject, relatively short in length, and reproduced in inexpensive format to allow timely and broad dissemination to researchers in aerospace history. Suggestions for additional publications in the Monographs in Aerospace History series are welcome and should be sent to Roger D. Launius, Chief Historian, Code ZH, National Aeronautics and Space Administration, Washington, DC, 20546. Previous publications in this series are:

Launius, Roger D. and Gillette, Aaron K. Compilers. *Toward a History of the Space Shuttle: An Annotated Bibliography.* (Monographs in Aerospace History, Number 1, 1992)

Launius, Roger D. and Hunley, J. D. Compilers. *An Annotated Bibliography of the Apollo Program.* (Monographs in Aerospace History, Number 2, 1994)

Launius, Roger D. *Apollo: A Retrospective Analysis.* (Monographs in Aerospace History, Number 3, 1994)

Hansen, James R. *Enchanted Rendezvous: John C. Houbolt and the Genesis of the Lunar-Orbit Rendezvous Concept.* (Monographs in Aerospace History, Number 4, 1995)

Gorn, Michael H. *Hugh L. Dryden's Career in Aviation and Space.* (Monographs in Aerospace History, No. 5, 1996).

Powers, Sheryll Goecke. *Women in Aeronautical Engineering at the Dryden Flight Research Center, 1946-1995.* (Monographs in Aerospace History, No. 6, 1997).

Portree, David S.F. and Trevino, Robert C. Compilers. *Walking to Olympus: A Chronology of Extravehicular Activity (EVA).* (Monographs in Aerospace History, No. 7, 1997).

Logsdon, John M. Moderator. *The Legislative Origins of the National Aeronautics and Space Act of 1958: Proceedings of an Oral History Workshop.* (Monographs in Aerospace History, No. 8, 1998).

Rumerman, Judy A. Compiler. *U.S. Human Spaceflights: A Record of Achievement, 1961-1998.* (Monographs in Aerospace History, No. 9, 1998).

Portree, David S.F. *NASA's Origins and the Dawn of the Space Age.* (Monographs in Aerospace History, No. 10, 1998).

Logsdon, John M. *Together in Orbit: The Origins of International Cooperation in the Space Station Program.* (Monographs in Aerospace History, No. 11, 1998).

Phillips, W. Hewitt. *Journey in Aeronautical Research: A Career at NASA Langley Research Center.* (Monographs in Aerospace History, No. 12, 1998).

Braslow, Albert L. *A History of Suction-Type Laminar-Flow Control with Emphasis on Flight Research.* (Monographs in Aerospace History, No. 13, 1999).

Logsdon, John M. Moderator. *Managing the Moon Program: Lessons Learned from Project Apollo* (Monographs in Aerospace History, No. 14, 1999).

Perminov, V. G. *The Difficult Road to Mars: A Brief History of Mars Exploration in the Soviet Union* (Monographs in Aerospace History, No. 15, 1999).